LEARNABILITY ISN'T ENOUGH

How to design apps
that are easy to use in *the long run,*
not just *the first run*

HANS VAN DE BRUGGEN

Learnability Isn't Enough: How to Design Apps That Are Easy to Use in the Long Run, Not Just the First Run

Copyright © 2023–2024 by Hans van de Bruggen

All rights reserved.

This publication is designed to provide accurate and authoritative information in regard to the subject matter covered. It is sold with the understanding that neither the author nor the publisher is engaged in rendering legal, investment, accounting or other professional services. While the publisher and author have used their best efforts in preparing this book, they make no representations or warranties with respect to the accuracy or completeness of the contents of this book and specifically disclaim any implied warranties of merchantability or fitness for a particular purpose. No warranty may be created or extended by sales representatives or written sales materials. The advice and strategies contained herein may not be suitable for your situation. You should consult with a professional when appropriate. Neither the publisher nor the author shall be liable for any loss of profit or any other commercial damages, including but not limited to special, incidental, consequential, personal, or other damages.

Paperback: 979-8-9888260-4-0   Hardcover: 979-8-9888260-8-8

Ebook: 979-8-9888260-6-4

Book Cover and Creative Direction by Hans van de Bruggen

Cover Illustration by Shyama Golden

Developmental Editing by James Robinson-Prior, Julie Meridian, and Maria Romanovsky

Editorial Review by Nicole Sholly

Line Editing by Dan Foster

Composition by Danielle Foster

Version 3.1 RC2 (2024)

To my incredible mom,
who taught me the meaning of the word "resiliency"

CONTENTS

PART II

PREFACE
About the book & its author

This book teaches you how to design apps so that they're easier to use in the long term.

So, who am I and what do I know about this subject? My name is Hans van de Bruggen, and I'm a Product Designer. I've been making websites since I was 12 years old, and built a website when I was 14 that helped to lift my family out of poverty. Since then, I've been fortunate to work alongside some of the best designers on the planet at large Silicon Valley companies (FAANG), tiny 1–3 designer startups, and everything in between. I've designed specialist tools used by small groups of professionals for hours each day, as well as work that has gone viral, being used by hundreds of millions of people across the globe (if you're curious, I keep a list on my website hansv.com). I've been interviewed as a subject matter expert by the New York Times, and design projects I've overseen have been featured in a number of major publications, including Wired, Variety, and Esquire.

Over the years, I've refined the techniques in this book with teams of varying sizes, experience levels, and industries. These have been battle-tested in many different contexts, which has led to my being asked to teach these techniques to others, and ultimately, to write about them. I've heard many success stories from folks who have leveraged these techniques, and after you've read this book, I hope to count you among them.

ACKNOWLEDGEMENTS

It takes a village to write a book. I've had an incredibly supportive group behind me, and it is now my privilege to be able to thank them. Each person here helped shape it into what you hold in your hands now.

Thank you to everyone who encouraged me to sit down and write this. In particular, thank you to Alia Kaussar, Ayoung Shim, Harrison Wheeler, Gordon Koo, and Tarang Gupta for the inspiration to include various stories.

Thank you to the truly stunning colleagues who played a role in supporting the exploration of these ideas, including Addison Kowalski, Amelie Wisniak, Becky Ingle, Carol Bang, Chris Fernandez, Cory Bates, David Vieyra, Herson Rodriguez, Ian McCarthy, Jason Huff, Jay Smith, Jessica Gaddis, Ji Yoon Ahn, John Wolanin, Kyna Payawal, Lea Ann Hutter, Marco Sevilla, Robinson Eaton, Ryan Day, Ryan Johnson, Ryan Reynolds, Sarah Beldo, Sarah Ohye, Vivian Urata, and Yevgeniy Brikman. In particular, I owe a deep debt of gratitude to Andrea Mangini and Steve Johnson for taking a chance on me. You gave me a front-row seat to what compassionate leadership looks like.

Thank you to the Beta readers and to everyone who was a sounding board to these ideas, including Abby Covert, Alex Kim, Andrea Aniceto-Chavez, Christina Choi, Christina Yang, Cleopatra Hornitzky, Danielle, Deborah Fellinger, Edi, Emily Lin, Fabio, Federico, Hailey, Helen, Ian and Zach, Janna Yang, Jared Spool, Jess Larson, Jia Ivey, Julie Kim, Karen Ueng, Katerina Lengold, Luc, Meg Qu, Moeez, Rokshana, Sazzad, Shajee, Stunji Alexandrova, Tatiana, Vaggos, Vivid Savitri, and Eli the cat. A special thank you to Rob Fitzpatrick, Devin Hunt, and the Write Useful Books community for their help in collecting and parsing this feedback.

Thank you to my book team, namely Julie Meridian (for helping me untangle this Gordian Knot), Maria Romanovsky (for your truly game-changing feedback), James Robinson-Prior @ Apress (for your early edits and continued help along the way), Dan Foster (for thinning the weeds), Danielle Foster (for your take on the book's layout), Nicole Sholly (for your help with structure and flow), and Shyama Golden (for your beautiful illustrations). I'm so glad we were able to work together.

Thank you to Mr. Brady (for fostering my love of computers), Mr. Dorsey (for putting books in my hands), and Ian Coyle (for giving me my first glimpse behind the curtain of the design world).

Thank you to my family: my parents, brothers, aunts, uncles, cousins, and grandparents who provided a loving environment growing up. That is a privilege I don't take for granted. I hope to see you all soon. A special thank you to my incredible mother, to whom this book is dedicated and who somehow raised four boys on her own.

Lastly, I want to thank interaction design pioneers like Don Norman, Jakob Nielsen (a hat tip to *Usability Engineering*), Bruce "Tog" Tognazzini, Alan Cooper, and others like them whose work has paved the way.

I should perhaps go farther, but that is as far as my memory will take me today. If your name managed to slip my mind, know that your contribution was no less valuable. For your help, I am in your debt.

PART I

1

INTRODUCTION:
TWO TYPES OF
"EASE OF USE"

While better learnability is valuable, it doesn't necessarily make an app easier to use day to day.

Surprisingly, it's often the reverse—things that make an app easier to figure out can actually make it more difficult to use overall. This point isn't immediately apparent to many folks, and I was no exception. For years, this was at the root of many issues with my own design work. But now that I know what to look for, I see this happening everywhere. It's extremely common, and often leads to angry users and wasted time. In the worst cases, it can even result in a failed product.

Thankfully, you can avoid all this once you know how.

This book will teach you how to design app interfaces that are easy to use in the long run, not just the first run. Ahead, you'll learn how to avoid the issue I just mentioned and achieve better results with less wasted time, effort, and user pain.

> *"Now that you've pointed it out, it seems crazy we haven't been doing this already."*
>
> —*My former product manager*

A mistake anyone can make

Learnability and usability are different things.

Unfortunately, they are often discussed interchangeably, with people tending to say that a change has made things "easier" when what they often mean is that it's "easier to figure out." But as mentioned a moment ago, it's possible for a learnability improvement to ultimately be *worse* for overall ease of use. In other words, *easier to learn* can mean *harder to use overall*.

When we forget to distinguish between learnability and usability, it can lead to incorrect priorities and false confidence. I've seen it happen everywhere from industry giants to the smallest startups. The way we use language often creates a barrier to making this distinction clear, so it's *absurdly* easy to get this wrong.

And when teams *do* get this wrong, the results can be disastrous.

In fact, while I was writing this book, a software update was released for Tesla vehicles that many drivers didn't like. The new interface moved some controls into more logical and easier-to-understand menus. But as a result, it now required 2–3 steps to access certain controls that used to be available with a single tap or swipe. It occurred to me that this fit the pattern. These issues resulted from the interface being made easier to learn at the cost of being harder to use day to day.

So, on a lark, I made a prototype showing how they might resolve many of these complaints by making a simple change. I proposed a straightforward way for drivers to add shortcuts back to the main screen. With this change, these common controls could once again be accessed with a single tap. This idea was really nothing extraordinary, but it made a specific and *targeted* change. With it, the interface would require less effort to use day to day while retaining all the learnability benefits provided by the new menu system.

I posted my proposal online and asked for feedback from owners. Unexpectedly, it quickly went viral and was shared and viewed hundreds of thousands of times in a matter of hours. Soon, Tesla news sites had written articles about it. To my surprise, one of these articles even prompted a response from CEO Elon Musk himself. Unfortunately, he took the position that the change wasn't necessary.

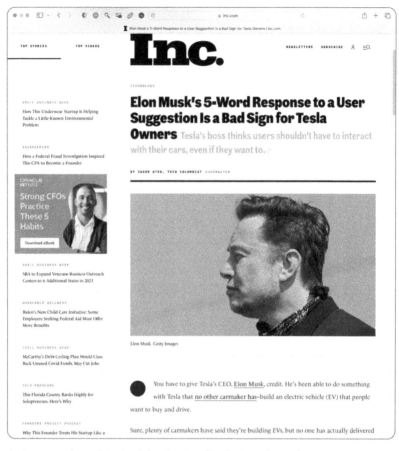

An *Inc.* magazine article about the situation. (Credit: Getty Images)

To say that this frustrated some people would be an understatement. The pushback he got from this was, at the time, the strongest reaction I had ever seen from the Tesla faithful. Some fans called him arrogant; others said the company had lost its way, and at least one owner sold their car and swore they'd never buy another vehicle from the brand again. A major magazine published an article about the backlash,[1] and a former presidential candidate even weighed in on the situation.

Yikes.

---

1. Aten, J. (2022, January 16). Elon Musk's 5-Word Response to a User Suggestion Is a Bad Sign for Tesla Owners. Inc.com. https://www.inc.com/jason-aten/elon-musks-5-word-response-to-a-user-suggestion-is-a-bad-sign-for-tesla-owners.html

Ultimately, three months later, the company did make the change. But in many ways, the damage to the brand had already been done.

Admittedly, the issue with this interface might seem obvious when we look at it through this framing. You might be tempted to write off design teams for being foolish enough to have made mistakes like these in the first place. But I believe these issues are the natural consequence of a larger issue with how we think about and discuss ease of use. This mistake often happens by default—it is *commonplace*.

Yet as mentioned earlier, when you know what to look for, you can often avoid these issues *before* users feel the resulting pain. This can spare you from the dramatic consequences that sometimes follow. With the tools in this book, you'll be able to make major design changes while minimizing your risk of user backlash like this.

Usability testing can be deceptive

These new tools provide insights that typically come later in the design process. This is helpful because our usual tools and processes will often leave gaps in our knowledge until *after* a product has shipped.

This first became clear to me a few years ago while I was working on a tool that healthcare professionals would use in hospitals. It was an app they would use in life-or-death situations, so I wanted to take every precaution to ensure that we did things right. We did extensive usability testing, and we occasionally had the chance to shadow users as they worked, as well. While walking with one of these users through a hospital, I heard them use an expression that was new to me. It was an expression that was commonly used in the stroke ward to communicate a sense of urgency:

"Time is brain."

That grabbed my attention. Here, every second wasted led to a worse outcome, so day-to-day efficiency was vital for these people. I suddenly wondered—how could we ensure we were doing a good job at this ahead of time, before we'd built anything?

I thought about the usability testing we were doing. It was the typical best practice of putting changes in front of people who had never seen them before, and asking ourselves questions like "Did they know what that meant?" and "Were they able to figure it out?" Whenever an interface made it through this process with few complaints, we would determine it to have successfully passed the usability test.

The issue, though, was because we were doing what we might call "first-look" usability testing, we were only ever able to get an initial reaction from these users. Even when we talked to users who knew an earlier version of the interface well, it could be tricky to get anything more than a first impression. Because we only gave them a short time to evaluate it, they had a hard time determining how comfortable it would be to use after some time had passed.

Usability tests are often learnability tests

It dawned on me that these weren't so much *usability* tests; they were *learnability* tests. We were only ever able to find out whether an interface was intuitive, with very little revealed about long-term ease of use until after it had been used for some time.

However, for many of these hospital users, learnability wasn't the main concern. In fact, it was the opposite—many of them would choose an interface that was *harder to learn* if it meant they could move with greater speed and fluidity when the time came. In practice, learning effort did matter to them, but not as much as the day-to-day effort of using it in the weeks, months, and years that followed.

Yet in "first-look" usability testing, we saw the same results as we always did. Users had tended to prefer the easier-to-learn options, and we'd concluded that they were therefore easier to use. But sometimes, what they chose turned out to be better for learnability but harder to use in the long term.

That was a problem—these tests were only telling us part of the story.

A usability blind spot

I wondered if I was missing something, so I went to see what the experts had to say. Eventually, I stumbled across this section on usability testing in the design classic *About Face*[2]:

> *Unfortunately, it's difficult to craft a test that assesses anything beyond first-time ease of learning. [...] [U]sability testing, by its nature, focuses on assessing a product's first-time use. It is often quite difficult (and always laborious) to measure how effective a solution is on its 50th use—in other words, for the most common target: the perpetual intermediate user. This is quite a conundrum when you are optimizing a design for intermediate or expert users.*
>
> *(emphasis mine)*

While the book recognized the value in looking beyond first impressions, it described the process as being "laborious" and "difficult". As a result, the advice tended to focus on assessing learnability.

This aligned with what I'd read elsewhere—it was the norm to focus on learnability. But I saw something a moment later that I did not expect. Elsewhere on that same page, the book described giving interface mockups to developers by printing them out, which hasn't been a best practice for decades. This was a valuable reminder that design methods continually evolve over time. With that in mind, I reasoned that there might be less painful techniques available to help with this today. (Thankfully, there are, and we'll look at them in depth in Chapter 4.)

We took a moment to reflect on what we'd learned. In the hospital, we had an audience that often valued speed and efficiency over learnability. But because we were focusing on "first-look" usability testing, problems with learnability were often caught while other issues were able to sneak through unnoticed.

---

2. About Face, by Alan Cooper, Reimann, R.; Cronin, D. & Noessel, C., 2014, pp. 139, 141.

It became clear that this was a blind spot. Yes, users often told us about day-to-day usability issues after using an interface for some time. But we were not doing anything in the initial design phase to spot these issues in advance. In fact, when I reflected on the usability testing I had done over the years with some truly world-class design teams, I couldn't identify a single time that we'd focused on trying to proactively spot issues with long-term ease of use. It simply wasn't a part of the process.

Designing for efficiency and comfort

Keeping an eye on long-term ease of use seemed important. Yet while we had great tools for figuring out whether things were easy to learn, I discovered I didn't even have concise language to describe all the effort of using an interface that somebody would experience *apart from the effort of learning it*.

We could see that there was effort involved in learning what to do, as well as effort that persisted even after figuring it out. It was common to focus on improving learnability. Perhaps there was also a way we could focus in on this "non-learning effort?"

With clearer language to describe this, my team and I believed we could discuss, understand, and reduce it more easily. I eventually settled on the term *UI Ergonomics*, as the New Oxford American Dictionary defined "ergonomic" as "relating to or designed for efficiency and comfort in the working environment."

This seemed to resonate with people. Those two things—an interface's overall *efficiency* and *comfort*—appeared to be essential components of this "non-learning effort." I should note that we're using the term "ergonomic" loosely since there may be marked differences between this and the traditional study of human factors. Yet for our purposes, the word has proven helpful as shorthand, as it seems to conjure images of unencumbered, graceful, fluid experiences designed to feel comfortable after many hours of use.

With this, I now had a simple way to discuss it with teammates and stakeholders. We could break *usability* into two pieces: *learning effort* and *ergonomic effort*.

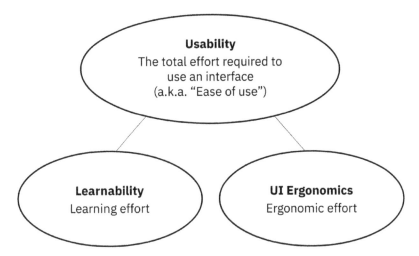

We split usability into two types of effort: learning effort and ergonomic effort.

Examples of learning effort and ergonomic effort

We can think of the difficulty of any task as a combination of both these types of effort. For example, picture someone who wants to get a snack from a vending machine each afternoon. They'll need to figure out how to use the machine to select the items they want. Yet even after they've gotten the hang of it, they'll still need to go through the routine of pushing the buttons correctly every time they want a snack. There is upfront (learning) effort, but there is also ongoing (ergonomic) effort.

To help illustrate, the following are examples of *learning effort*. These center around the effort of figuring out what to do and how to do it:

- Which button should I be looking for?
- Will this function do what I want?
- What do I do next?

And here are some examples of *ergonomic effort*. These center around effort that doesn't go away, no matter how well you learn it:

- The button I need to hit is small, which makes it harder to aim for.

- It takes a moment for the device to show that it received my input, which throws me off when I'm trying to move quickly.

- The information I need is in a different location each time, which makes it difficult to spot.

What this book will cover

With the introduction out of the way, let's take a look at what you can expect in the pages ahead. This book focuses on the vital role of *ergonomic effort* in designing easy-to-use apps. This is a topic that doesn't often get much dedicated attention, so to keep things focused, there won't be a deep exploration of learnability, capabilities, or product–market fit. Instead, along the way, you'll see how UI Ergonomics intertwines with other factors like these in products that users truly love.

This book is a *practical guide*. While there are different ways you can break usability apart,[3] splitting usability in this way unlocks a set of powerful and transformative tools. Throughout this book, I'll walk you through these tools and show how they can help you do the following:

- Spot many interface issues proactively that typically only get fixed after users complain

- Make a better case to teammates and stakeholders for impactful changes that often get dismissed as being "unintuitive" or "insignificant"

---

3. Breaking usability into two pieces on the basis of effort appears to be novel. Taking usability apart certainly isn't new—most notably, Jakob Nielsen and Ben Shneiderman separate usability into five pieces (Learnability, Speed/Efficiency, Retention/ Memorability, Accuracy/Errors, and Subjective Satisfaction). However, while it's helpful to use this five-part approach, I've found there is real value in differentiating purely on the basis of the type of effort required. In the approach introduced here, these two types of effort have unique distinguishing attributes, which makes it possible to draw useful contrasts. Both of these approaches have different merits and can be applied to gain different insights; this is meant to augment, not replace.

- Make larger redesign projects less risky by avoiding interface changes that upset, frustrate, and drive away your most invested users
- Make design priorities clearer by comparing your interface to others in terms of the effort required

Part I

As you've just seen, Part I of this book introduces the idea of dividing usability into *learning* and *ergonomic* effort. Through this lens, the rest of Part I covers three main topics. First, it gives you a simple visual for quickly communicating why certain changes are more impactful than they might seem, which makes it easier for you to get buy-in from those you work with. Second, it shows you how you can make changes to interfaces without frustrating your existing user base. And third, it provides ways to effectively measure the effort often missed by "first-look" usability testing, which helps you to overcome the blind spot mentioned earlier. I recommend reading these chapters in order as they build on each other.

Part II

Part II of this book gives you a guide to the system I use throughout the design process that will help you spot ergonomic improvements in advance. This is called the CUPID System, which grew out of seven years of detailed notes on common sources of ergonomic effort. You can use this as a "preflight checklist" for your projects, and to help you give better feedback when reviewing work with your team. Chapters 6–10 contain many examples of specific improvements you can make to enhance the long-term usability of your app. These chapters can be read at any time, but it's best to read Chapter 5 first.

Appendices

Lastly, the book includes several additional tools in the appendices. Appendix A introduces a tool called the Usability Matrix. This gives you a new way to compare interfaces and enables you to make clearer decisions about where to focus your design efforts. Appendix B covers the Product Pyramid, which uses this framework to help you understand user behavior as it relates to your app. Finally, Appendix C includes the CUPID Cheat Sheets, which make it easier to use the CUPID System with your team.

As designers, we build tools to help users reach their goals with less pain and effort. The tools in this book are here to help you do the same.

KEY POINTS TO REMEMBER

In this book, we split "ease-of-use" into two distinct types of effort. *Learning effort* is the upfront effort it takes to become familiar with an interface; *ergonomic effort* is all the effort that remains, which persists long after it has been learned. Often, ergonomic effort is revealed through user feedback after people have had a chance to use it for a while. Instead, with this book, you'll see how to quickly spot opportunities and fix issues like these in advance. This is a *superpower*, as it allows you to move more swiftly while sparing users from much of the pain that is normally inherent to this process.

In other words, you'll be able to ship better products with fewer complaints that need to be addressed later. This makes users happier while increasing your bandwidth, giving you a huge advantage.

TRY THIS

- When you hear someone describe something as being "easier," ask yourself, "Do they mean it's easier *to learn*?" You'll start to see just how common it is to talk about *ease of use* and *ease of learning* as if they were the same thing. This should help underscore how often ergonomic effort gets overlooked and why paying special attention is so important.

- **Try to spot the difference between learning effort and ergonomic effort in the wild.** When you have trouble with a task, ask yourself, "Would this be any easier if I knew this process better? Or is the task *inherently* tricky?" Remember that problems with ergonomics don't go away with time and experience—these difficulties are inherent to the task. The more practice you get with this, the less trouble you will have catching these kinds of issues.

UP NEXT

Even if you believe in the importance of good ergonomics, your team or stakeholders may still need some convincing.

As we've discussed, an interface can do well in "first-look" usability testing even when it has severe issues with ergonomics. That makes things difficult—you may need to be able to explain why an interface that passed this testing is not actually the "easier" option in the long term.

This can feel like an impossible task, so being able to communicate this point with clarity is important. Next chapter, we'll build upon what was covered here with a visual tool to help you clarify and get the support of your team. ⊙

2

HOW TO HELP YOUR TEAM PRIORITIZE LONG-TERM VS. SHORT-TERM USABILITY

The previous chapter discussed how we can break "ease of use" into two types of effort: "learning effort" (the effort it takes to learn how to use something, such as figuring out which buttons to push) and "ergonomic effort" (all the non-learning effort required to use something, such as the work required to actually press each button).

Learning effort and *ergonomic effort* are inherently quite different, and as you'll soon see, this can help us narrow in on more impactful changes depending on the context. Unfortunately, many ergonomic improvements aren't immediately apparent as priorities to stakeholders. That can make it challenging to get support for prioritizing "smaller" changes like smoothing out interface stutters or changing the locations of buttons. Instead, these things often take a backseat to getting new functionality out the door or making things more intuitive.

Frequently, however, these small changes can have a dramatic impact on user happiness. In this chapter, you'll see how ergonomic effort continues to add up over time for all users, regardless of experience level. This will help you to clearly demonstrate to stakeholders the impact of these changes, and where they will be the most effective (making it much easier to get buy-in).

Thankfully, this is easier than it might sound. I was once following up with a coworker who had presented her work for feedback from the team at a design crit. She was designing an internal tool that her users depended on to do their job each day. This tool was the backbone of their work—nearly everyone who used this app spent most of their workday using it.

I was designing an internal tool for another team, and our users had similarly heavy use cases. It struck me that some of the simple ergonomic improvements our team had made could also make a big difference to the product she was overseeing. When I told her about how delighted our users were by these changes, she asked me a question:

> *"I'm curious...How did you know this was something your users needed? And how did you manage to convince your team to prioritize this?"*

I showed her a diagram that I use with my teams that helps to visualize why these kinds of things were worth prioritizing. It takes less than 10 seconds to draw, but I've seen it make all the difference when trying to build consensus. Let's explore it now, and afterward, I'll also point you toward additional tools you can use if your team still needs more convincing.

A diagram for showing different types of effort over time

To get the support of our teams and stakeholders, quickly communicating the differences between *learning effort* and *ergonomic effort* is key. Here's the diagram I use to show how each type of effort changes over the time spent with an interface:

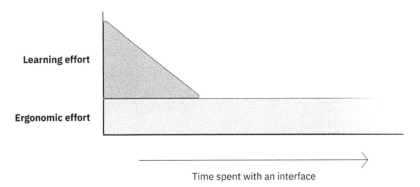

Time spent with an interface

A graph of the effort required to use an interface over time.

As a diagram, it's a bit of an oversimplification, but it works for our purposes. If you wanted to be accurate, the slope for learning effort would most likely scoop down and to the right, never quite touching zero, with some "lumpiness" to account for forgetfulness. But for our needs, a simple wedge clearly conveys what matters here, and it's easier to sketch out quickly when discussing with your team or stakeholders.

In simple terms, this diagram shows that learning effort tends to go down over time, but ergonomic effort does not. Let's walk through the logic.

Learning the process vs. doing the process

Remember, you can find these two types of effort in any task. For example, think about the task of making dinner. It takes effort to get the hang of preparing a new recipe. But even after learning it, it will still take effort to go through the process of making it each time. There is upfront effort, and there is also ongoing effort. With that, let's look at the diagram.

Learning effort fades

When somebody starts using an interface, they are at the beginning of the learning phase. As they figure things out and develop muscle memories, they're faced with fewer and fewer things left to learn, so we can expect the amount of effort they spend on learning to gradually move closer to zero over time. Once they've learned it well enough, this effort may have a negligible impact on their day-to-day use.

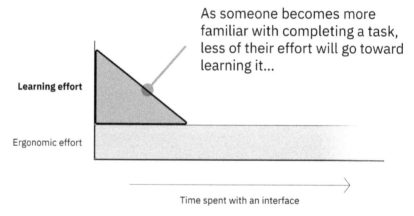

As someone becomes more familiar with completing a task, less of their effort will go toward learning it...

Learning effort

Ergonomic effort

Time spent with an interface

Learning effort is highest at the beginning but reduces over time.

In the beginning, users need to figure out how to use the interface before they can get any value out of it. This imperative, combined with the learning effort required, is a draw on their attention. This can distract them from the pain of ergonomic effort until later. That may be why users at this early stage tend to provide feedback with a strong focus on learnability issues, only to notice ergonomic issues later.

Of course, most users will never get to the point where they know absolutely *everything* about *every* interaction, but that's not what's important. The point is that the trend is the same for everyone: for a given interface, users have more to learn at the beginning, and over time will tend to face less and less remaining learning effort. In other words, *as experience increases, learning effort decreases.*

Ergonomic effort sticks around

However, unlike learning effort, *ergonomic effort never goes away* because every interaction requires manual and cognitive effort to perform. In other words, the effort required to locate and push a button is an inherent part of the interaction itself and can never be eliminated entirely. In order for a user to have pushed a button, they must in fact push it—this effort sticks around.

This establishes an unavoidable minimum level of effort. As long as there are steps to take, this effort must be present.

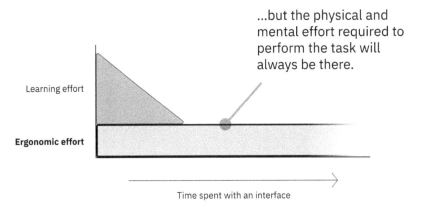

...but the physical and mental effort required to perform the task will always be there.

Ergonomic effort is persistent, and as a result, it continues to add up over time (forever).

Since this effort never goes away, time is a critical component. As learning effort is felt less and less by a user over time, more and more of the friction they notice will instead come from ergonomic effort. It's the part that they're stuck with, and it keeps adding up. Over time, it gradually becomes the source of friction users care most about as they use an interface.

As a result, this isn't just a source of friction. For many users, it's the *primary* source of friction. To improve usability for them, we must address this effort specifically.

For a professional tool used for long periods of time, like the ones my coworker and I were building, the overall ergonomic effort involved may become *immense*. So, while it can be hard to evaluate this effort using "first-look" usability testing, it's something that users can become highly attuned to over time—we'll explore that more in the next chapter.

But while experienced users can become deeply familiar with this, the reality is that *all* users deal with this effort, whether or not they notice it yet. Although a less experienced user is likely to focus on the pain of learning at the beginning, they're enduring ergonomic effort either way. They will still face the effort inherent to issuing commands, even if they're preoccupied with figuring out which ones to use. Ultimately, because this friction is universal, it means that improvements can benefit *every* user.

How to communicate this with your team and stakeholders

If you have a good sense of how to use this diagram when talking with coworkers, feel free to skip ahead. Otherwise, here's a step-by-step walkthrough:

1. Draw a simple graph with a vertical and horizontal axis and label them "effort" and "time," respectively.
2. Draw a short, wide rectangle at the bottom of the graph to indicate ergonomic effort. To do this, I recommend drawing a horizontal line and quickly shading the area underneath. Leaving the right side of this area open helps to underscore that the effort is ongoing.
3. Draw a triangle wedge on top of this, sloping down from the left edge, to indicate the amount of learning effort. If possible, do this with a different color for extra clarity.
4. Tell your coworker, "This is a diagram of the effort required to use an interface over time."

5. Point to the wedge and say, "This wedge represents the amount of effort it takes to learn how to use an interface, like the effort of figuring out which buttons to push. We can call this 'learning effort.'" Write out the words "learning effort" and show how there's more to learn at the beginning, which goes away gradually as a person becomes more familiar with how to use something.

6. Point to the shaded rectangle underneath the wedge, and say, "This area represents all the effort of using an interface apart from the effort of learning it, like the effort it takes to actually push each button. We can call this 'ergonomic effort.' This effort is a part of every interaction." Write out the words "ergonomic effort" and show how this effort does not go away.

7. Emphasize this further by saying, "Because this effort doesn't go away, it will continue to add up over time for all users. So, the more our interface is used, the more important it is to reduce this."

8. Lastly, if you are building an app that individual users will spend a lot of time in, such as a tool used by professionals at their jobs, emphasize just how long this bar can get when used day after day for weeks, months, and even years. When I talk about this, I will sometimes extend the area that shows ergonomic effort further to the right or draw an arrow to show that it keeps going. This helps paint a clearer picture of just how impactful this effort can be over time.

A quick walkthrough of this diagram is enough to make the importance of this clear to most teammates and stakeholders (it has never failed me, personally). But if your audience remains unmoved by this, Chapter 4 offers several ways to help you quantify the amount of ergonomic effort present. In addition, Appendix A shows how to use a Usability Matrix to visually demonstrate usability strengths and weaknesses between two interfaces.

Focus on how much experience users will get, not on how much experience they currently have

Earlier, we discussed how ergonomic effort is universal and that every user can benefit when you improve it. But it's not uncommon for valuable changes to be written off as only helpful to "experts" or "power users," so you'll want to know how to manage this kind of pushback.

This belief may be common because requests for these improvements will often come from users with a lot of experience. But these users aren't the only ones dealing with this effort—they simply notice it while everyone else is still distracted by learning effort.

This provides valuable insight. These users allow us to "see the future"—to spot the friction that might not yet have been noticed by everyone but that exists for all users.

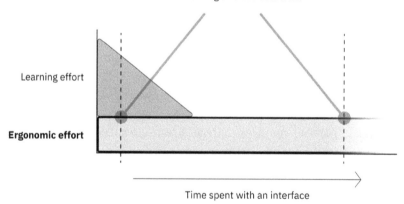

For a given interface, ergonomic effort is the same on day 1 as it is on day 50. While you'll often get requests for ergonomic improvements from more experienced users, these improvements can help all users.

As an example, let's go back to the idea of making dinner each day. When someone is learning to cook, they'll often be focused on how much of each ingredient they need to use and how to prepare each one. But as they get more comfortable with the process, they'll start noticing other points of friction. They might realize that their measuring cup often spills water when they pour it or that their knife goes dull quickly. These were always points of friction, but they often go unnoticed until later.

Remember this when you hear requests for ergonomic improvements from users with a bit of experience. They might be the only ones currently asking for a better measuring cup or cutting board, but these are often things that will help everyone using them.

Users will get more experience with high-overlap elements

Most teams don't have unlimited resources, so it's valuable to know how to prioritize these improvements. Always remember that ergonomic effort adds up with use. As a result, a great starting point is to focus on the interface elements that will get used most often.

Start by identifying which parts of the app get used in multiple ways across multiple workflows. In the previous example, having access to a better measuring cup will reduce the effort of making many recipes, not just one. Interfaces work the same way, with many workflows centering around common elements like toolbars, status indicators, and navigation systems. But you can also find high-use interactions specific to the workflows, themselves, such as the steps needed to go to and from a given screen or to enter and exit a mode. Because these get used much more than other parts of an interface, it makes them a prime target for ergonomic improvements.

Keep an eye open for these kinds of high-overlap interface elements in your app. I call these "conduits" for short, but feel free to use whatever term makes the most sense to you and your team. When reviewing work with your team, call these out to ensure they receive the necessary attention.

Users will get even more experience when they have heavy use cases

In addition, consider users with heavier use cases. While they can sometimes have needs that are more specialized, the elements they interact with *the most* still tend to be the same as those used by everyone else; they just use them more frequently. A navigation bar will be used a lot by everyone, for example, but a more demanding use case acts as a multiplier.

People who use professional tools at work are a prime example. Often, they'll spend hours inside these apps each workday. So if you're building professional tools, UI Ergonomics are incredibly important—*especially* in the high-usage parts of the interface.

After discussing this, my coworker could see why ergonomic improvements would be so impactful to the tool she was building. Her users spent hours inside the app each day, so this effort was a major part of their experience. This diagram enabled her to quickly make this point to her team and stakeholders, which helped her to get these improvements prioritized.

KEY POINTS TO REMEMBER

We can evaluate whether a painpoint is inherently temporary, or whether it will continue to affect users over time. This is the crux of the approach we're exploring—determining which sources of effort a user can learn to overcome, and which they'll be stuck with. This gives us a way to identify long-term painpoints well in advance of shipping a product.

Ergonomic effort is baked in when a product ships—it can't be reduced by a user, so it adds up endlessly as time goes on. As a result, improving it in frequently used parts of the interface can greatly reduce the overall effort required. This is especially true for heavy use cases.

It's also important to remember that these improvements aren't just for "power users." This effort is present for everyone who uses a particular feature, whether or not they notice it right away.

As a result, reducing ergonomic effort for the most frequently used parts of an interface helps ensure the greatest benefit for the greatest number. Users with heavier use cases will simply notice these improvements earlier.

TRY THIS

- **Use the diagram presented in this chapter to create a shared mental model with your team and stakeholders.** See the step-by-step walkthrough in the "How to communicate this with your team and stakeholders" section if you need help.

- **Prioritize ergonomic improvements in the parts of your app that get the most use overall. The more often a given element is used, the more impactful it will be to improve it.** That makes more fundamental elements like buttons and status indicators especially important, so it can be valuable to start by focusing on your design system. Apart from that, identify the interactions and workflows that are used the most—check your usage metrics or implement click tracking if you need help nailing this down. Use the CUPID System as described in Chapter 5 to quickly find improvements.

- **When designing a new feature, find the interactions that will get used the most by asking, "Which steps are *always required* to complete this process?"** Often, these are steps at the beginning or the end of the process, such as opening and closing a modal, entering and exiting a mode, or going to and from a specific screen. There are often required steps in the middle, too, such as entering information or reading a status label. Identify the steps that are necessary *every time* to know what to focus on.

continues

- **Invest more heavily in improving ergonomics when a large group of your users is expected to have a heavy use case.** With professional tools, don't be meek about this—I've found the best results when optimizing all but the least-used functions. By focusing on how much experience a set of users *will get* instead of how much they *currently have*, you can help deliver what they need before they ask for it.

- **Listen to ergonomic concerns from users who have a bit of experience.** Remember that these users can help you spot ergonomic improvements before everyone else. They don't need to be "power users"—their experience with the feature in question matters more than their overall app experience.

UP NEXT

It's not hard to imagine folks either shooting down an interface tweak or dismissing strong user pushback with the phrase "Users hate change." What I've found, though, is that users don't have a problem with interface changes in and of themselves. Rather, they are particularly sensitive to the *type* of changes made. Understanding the role that UI Ergonomics play in this can enable you to make changes quickly while keeping users happy. →

3

HOW TO MAKE
CHANGES TO
YOUR INTERFACE
WITHOUT UPSETTING
YOUR USERS

If you've worked as a product designer for any amount of time, you've probably heard the expression, "Users hate change." It's often used as an excuse to leave things the way they are when there is a fear of disappointing longtime users. The implication is that change is inherently risky, so it's best to not rock the boat. And when changes do get made, the phrase also gets trotted out as an excuse when users don't like the new changes. This allows teams to shift the blame onto users and write off their complaints as simply the cost of doing business. After all, they say, "If you want to make an omelet, you have to break a few eggs."

What this conveniently ignores, though, are all the app updates that users *genuinely love*. People delight in getting more for less. In an interface, this often comes down to being able to get a desired result with less effort.

The trick is knowing how to make improvements to one type of effort without creating setbacks in another. In this chapter, we'll explore how you can update your app with confidence while minimizing your risk of backlash. To get there, we'll start by looking at how the act of learning a new way of doing things creates an expectation in our users (that doesn't always get met).

Learning is an investment users make

Learning a new way of completing a task is an investment. This is because we all have a natural, often subconscious, tendency to minimize the total effort we spend (for more on this, see Appendix B). It takes additional effort to figure out a new way of completing a task, so for this to feel worthwhile, we must believe that doing so will reduce our total effort over time.

In other words, when we relearn how to do something we do often, we are typically endeavoring to exchange additional learning effort for reduced ergonomic effort.

For example, imagine that when someone first started with an app, they used a multi-step wizard to walk them through a common process. This was easy to figure out but required a large number of inputs across several screens each time. Eventually, they relearn how to complete the process using a few keyboard shortcuts. They already knew how to do this with the multi-step wizard, but by investing more effort into learning another method, they save a considerable amount of ergonomic effort over time. The longer they will be doing this, the more effort they will save overall.

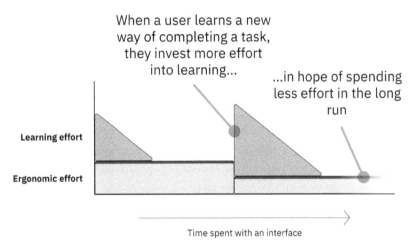

Users will spend more effort to learn a new way of doing something to reduce their total effort over time.

A redesigned interface adds effort that must be offset

However, when an interface is redesigned, some amount of new learning is typically not optional—it is *required* to be able to continue using the product.

Users want a good exchange, so there is an expectation that the redesigned interface will reduce the total effort needed in return. But as we've seen in Chapter 1, this doesn't always happen. Because there is a natural tendency to confuse learnability with ease of use, a redesigned interface will often reduce the amount of learning effort needed while inadvertently *increasing* the ergonomic effort needed.

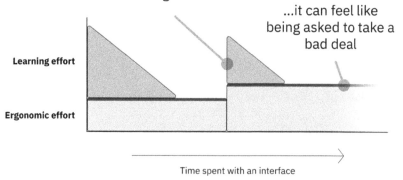

When a redesigned interface reduces learning effort but increases ergonomic effort...

...it can feel like being asked to take a bad deal

Learning effort

Ergonomic effort

Time spent with an interface

When a user is asked to spend more overall effort than before, it can be very frustrating.

This can be hugely problematic for existing users. People become increasingly familiar with the ergonomic effort required as they gain experience. As a result, when they discover that a redesigned interface has worse ergonomics, they can feel like they're being asked to spend more effort than is necessary. They know a better option exists.

It's a bit like being put in a class to relearn how to do something in exchange for less pay—it's a *bad deal* and can even feel a bit insulting.

In plain English, learnability is important for newer users. But if there's a process someone already completes a hundred times a day, making it easier to figure out isn't going to help them much. And if you require them to relearn how to do this in a way that isn't as efficient or comfortable as before, they're not going to be happy.

That is why it's ultimately so important to keep a close eye on the amount of ergonomic effort your interface requires. Because it continues to add up over time, it's this effort—*specifically*—that is what determines a user's efficiency and comfort long-term. It's vital to ensure that it stays the same or gets lower from one version to the next.

Redesigned with *better* ergonomics
Loved & appreciated by experienced users

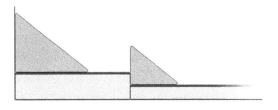

 Redesigned with *same* ergonomics
Additional learning is annoying, but temporary

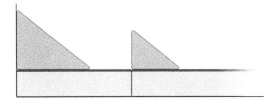

 Redesigned with *worse* ergonomics
Can make experienced users VERY upset

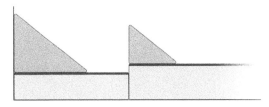

While new users care about the amount of learning effort required, more experienced users care more about ergonomic effort. Because of this, they can become frustrated when the amount of ergonomic effort required increases.

Providing the paths of least effort

Naturally, you'll want your interfaces to be as easy as possible for both new and existing users. But different approaches will often have inescapable tradeoffs between each type of effort. As a result, instead of relying on one approach to completing a task, it's often better to provide multiple options.

Here's the story of how I learned this the hard way and how you can avoid making the same mistake I did.

I was working on a tool with a filter-based search interface inherited from a framework we used. It was entirely keyboard driven, which meant that if a user wanted to apply a filter to their search, they would need to type it into the search field. As you'd expect, this made it tricky to figure out how to use it, as the available filter options didn't readily present themselves. Users either needed to bring up the list of filters as a reference or, more commonly, use a guess-and-check approach. Predictably, users had difficulty getting up to speed with the interface. It had problems with learnability.

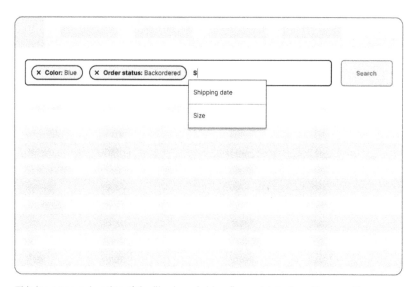

This is an approximation of the "keyboard-driven" search interface. Because the available filters aren't immediately apparent, a user is typing "S" to see all possible filters starting with that letter.

Knowing this, I redesigned the interface using a more self-evident graphical approach. I moved the filters into a set of menus so that users could quickly see the available options. Ultimately, this was validated in "first-look" usability testing. Our redesigned interface performed substantially better with new users when compared to the original. We saw this as the green light to build and deploy this new search interface.

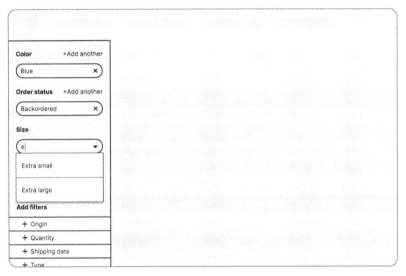

This is an approximation of the "graphical" search interface. Here, users can see all available filters, select the ones they want, then choose their desired filter terms.

A usability catch-22

But a few days after we had rolled out the new interface, many of our existing users were frustrated. While the new version was indeed easier to learn, these users said it required more effort to use each day than the previous keyboard-driven version. A surprising number of our users had memorized the search filters they used most often. They told us they'd enjoyed how the previous interface let them complete their searches using just a few keystrokes. This new interface was still fully accessible with a keyboard, but it now required many more inputs than before. This was problematic.

By now, you may have spotted the pattern. While this new graphical interface was a real improvement for newer users, it was a frustrating setback for many existing users. After using it in their regular work for a few days, many longtime users discovered they strongly preferred the previous interface. This was a classic case of a redesigned interface being easier to learn, but harder to use long-term.

We felt stuck in a catch-22. Even if we made the keyboard-driven approach easier to learn, it was inherently harder to figure out than the more intuitive graphical approach. But the same was true in reverse: even with improvements, the graphical approach was likely to always be less ergonomic than the keyboard-driven approach.

Choosing one method over another meant we would compromise either learning effort or ergonomic effort.

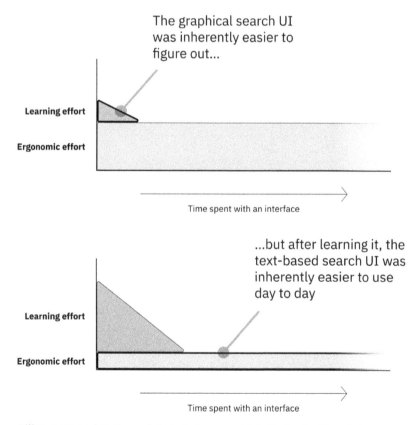

Different approaches to completing a task can provide better levels of learning or ergonomic effort. Choosing one over another can feel like making a difficult tradeoff.

Providing two approaches

It started to dawn on me—my goal wasn't to find an "ideal" solution, it was to optimize both of these factors. In other words, each of these types of effort was important for different reasons. This meant that the best way to optimize for these factors might be to tackle them independently, with a *learnable* path and an *ergonomic* path.

It occurred to me that this is a bit like *Moneyball*. In the movie, instead of looking for star players who each had a broad set of skills, they focused their resources on finding individual players who had specific skills they wanted on the team. For us as designers, it's a similar situation. Instead of trying to find the "best" single solution, our *actual* goal is to optimize both types of effort.

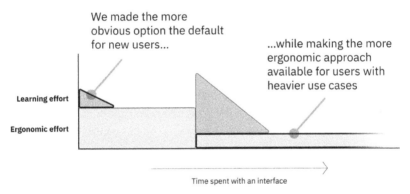

We made the more obvious option the default for new users...

...while making the more ergonomic approach available for users with heavier use cases

Learning effort

Ergonomic effort

Time spent with an interface

Building a single "perfect" solution is less important than providing access to a learnable option and an ergonomic option. If you're unable to combine these benefits into a single approach, then two approaches may be preferable.

Thankfully, in this case, we quickly solved the issue by providing an optional setting to restore the keyboard-driven search interface. New users would get the easier-to-learn interface by default, while a more ergonomic method was available for folks with more experience and heavier use cases.

How to make better interface changes

I've chosen this last example because it was easier to demonstrate visually. But you can usually find success without building two separate interfaces, as we did here. Most often, you can optimize for both types of effort as easily as pairing an intuitive control with a shortcut. It's the same basic principle—one path is more learnable, while the other is more ergonomic.

To complete a given task, every interface has what we can call a *Most Learnable Path (MLP)* and a *Most Ergonomic Path (MEP)*. The most learnable method may not be very ergonomic, and vice-versa. But from the perspective of your users, what matters is that you provide them with the best MLP and MEP you can. These might be completely different paths through the interface, but each one is serving a distinct set of needs.

MLP & MEP: Ways to make things easier for everyone

Here's a rundown of some ways we can leverage this to design interfaces that are easy up front and in the long term.

- **The Most Learnable Path (MLP):** Make things easy to figure out by default. The job of the MLP is to quickly get users to the point they can complete the task. It doesn't need to be the most efficient method. What matters is that they can get any functionality out of it at all, so you want to get them over this line as quickly as possible. In graphical interfaces, this is often done using a button or menu option that's easy to find and understand. Make your MLP as ergonomic as possible *without compromising learnability.*

- **The Most Ergonomic Path (MEP):** As we saw earlier, it's important for the MEP to remain the same or improve from one version to the next. "Invisible" shortcuts (meaning those that don't appear on the surface of the UI) are especially helpful for this. Common examples include shortcut keys, gestures, command palettes, voice commands, etc. Because they aren't tied to the UI, it makes them more resilient to UI changes. These are especially helpful for frequent actions, so try not to think of these as being optional. Save your easiest shortcuts for the most common interactions. Lastly, an MEP doesn't need to be as easy to learn as the default option, but remember that users can only benefit from ergonomic methods they can figure out. Make these as learnable as possible *without compromising ergonomics.*

In general, when designing processes, try to reduce the number of steps that are always required. Allow users to set defaults to skip steps they'd otherwise be required to take every time. For common processes, review which steps will always be required and try to pair *each one* with an accelerator (often, this can be as simple as letting a user swipe the screen or press Return to go on to the next step).

While shortcuts can be effective at reducing ergonomic effort, you should remember that long-term ease of use comes down to more than just that. Clear typography, fewer distractions, inputs with predictable outcomes, and more all have a measurable lasting effect. See the CUPID System overview in Chapter 5 for a guide to finding these improvements.

How to ensure ergonomics continue to improve, step-by-step

Lastly, here's a process you can use to ensure that ergonomic effort doesn't get worse for a given interaction from one version to the next:

1. **When making a change, identify several approaches to solving the problem.** If you're redesigning an interface, including the current approach in this list is crucial. Doing so ensures you are comparing your options against the current baseline.

2. **Do a quick CUPID exercise.** At this early stage, you're looking to catch bigger issues, so you don't need to be as thorough as later on. We'll look at this in Chapter 5.

3. **Determine which of these approaches offers a better MLP.** Most often, this is the approach you believe is the most *learnable*, inherently.

4. **Determine which of these approaches offers a better MEP.** Most often, this is the approach you believe is the most *ergonomic*, inherently.

5. **If these are both the same approach, you've found your winner.**

Otherwise:

6. **Combine the most learnable and most ergonomic options into a single approach that has the advantages of each.** This won't always be possible, but when it is, it can be ideal.

Otherwise:

7. **Offer both solutions, with the more learnable option as the default.** For single-step interactions, this often means pairing a more obvious control with an accelerator shortcut. For more complex interactions, like the search example we saw earlier, your best bet may be to offer both interfaces. This requires more of an investment, so it's best suited for situations where one of the options has already been built.

Combined, these techniques help you to ensure your interface becomes easier over time, for all users.

KEY POINTS TO REMEMBER

Learnability is vital for new users. But to keep existing users happy, ensuring that ergonomic effort never goes up is crucial.

As discussed, when a user learns a new way of doing something, they spend additional effort up front to try to save effort in the long run. This creates a give-and-take between learning effort and ergonomic effort.

So when a user knows an interface well and it gets redesigned, they face a new spike in learning effort. In return for this, they want to receive a lower effort baseline than they had before. *This doesn't always happen*, so paying special attention to this is essential.

By keeping an eye on your MEP, you can avoid changes that make things harder for your existing users. And when you know how to optimize both the MLP and MEP, you can ensure that things will continue to get easier for everyone, now and into the future.

TRY THIS

- **When you're working on a feature, identify the Most Learnable Path (MLP) and the Most Ergonomic Path (MEP).** In the example we looked at in this chapter, the graphical search interface offered the MLP, while the keyboard-driven interface offered the MEP. Use the advice in this chapter to ensure that both of these elements continue to improve from one version to the next.

- **Try to offer redundancy for your MEPs.** The most ergonomic option available often depends on the user and the context. As a result, giving users multiple accelerators can help them avoid needing to use a less ergonomic method. Voice controls might be highly ergonomic, for example. But if a user is unable to speak for one reason or another, they lose this option. Ensuring that multiple ergonomic paths are available makes it so users are less likely to get stuck using a substantially worse option.

- **In order to reduce a user's *overall* effort, try to reserve the most ergonomic shortcuts for the most common interactions.** For example, let's imagine that swiping left or right on an item on the page allows users to trigger an action. But suppose it's more common to navigate forward or back between pages. In that case, it may make more sense to allow users to navigate by swiping *anywhere* on the page and use a different shortcut to trigger the command for the item instead.

- **Consider "invisible" accelerators (like shortcut keys, gestures, command palettes, voice commands, and scriptable endpoints) for your most important interactions.** These provide a way of future-proofing the interface so that commands can continue to be triggered regardless of where buttons may be moved in future revisions. This provides somewhat of a safeguard against increases in ergonomic effort from one version to the next.

UP NEXT

As we've just discussed, keeping an eye on the ergonomic effort in your interface is essential. Now, we'll explore three techniques you can use to evaluate this. Combining these with traditional "first-look" usability testing can help you get a more comprehensive look at the usability of an interface. ⊙→

4

HOW TO ASSESS DAY-TO-DAY EASE OF USE, BEYOND LEARNABILITY

Earlier in this book, I told the story of how I was working on an app for hospital workers. Every moment mattered crucially to these users, so I wanted to ensure that the interface would stay out of their way as much as possible in their day-to-day work.

As time went on, I wondered, "Why aren't we giving UI Ergonomics the same scrutiny as we give to learnability? Why isn't this evaluation an expected and regular part of the process?" Even when we asked our most experienced users for feedback, they were typically given so little time with the interface that we only ever tended to catch the biggest, most glaring issues. But as we've seen, users often become hyperaware of ergonomic effort once they're beyond the learning phase. We really need to catch not only the *most obvious* issues, but also those that are *least obvious* (and everything in between).

At this point, we've talked about how valuable it can be to keep an eye on ergonomic effort, and you may be wondering how best to measure this. Thankfully, we have options.

Three methods for determining the amount of ergonomic effort in interfaces

At times, it may be most valuable to get precise measurements or qualitative input from users. But it's also possible to make a good estimate of an interface's ergonomic effort on your own. We'll look at ways to do all these things using the three techniques I've found most helpful for my own work.

As this chapter goes into some detail about how to use these techniques, you may want to start by skimming through it to get a sense of the options available to you. When you're ready to use these, you can return to use this chapter as a detailed reference guide.

Get a more robust view of overall usability

A quick word about "first-look" usability testing. To be clear, the typical practice of putting a new interface in front of users who have never seen it is still as important as ever. It's a key tool for validating whether an interface is easy to learn.

The techniques we're about to examine are meant to *complement* this testing, not replace it. When you combine these techniques with "first-look" usability testing, you will get a clearer picture of the overall usability of an interface *in its entirety*.

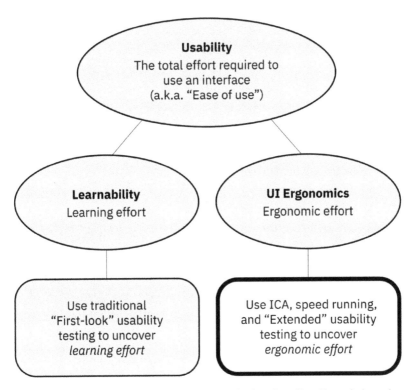

"First-look" usability testing is excellent for assessing learning effort. The techniques in this chapter help you assess ergonomic effort.

Because this book is focused on ergonomic effort, we won't be exploring "first-look" usability testing in any depth here. These days, most designers have experience with watching users working through tasks in a new interface. But if you want more information on this, the Nielsen Norman Group has some excellent resources available for free on their website (nngroup.com).

TECHNIQUE 1

Interaction Cost Analysis (ICA)

One of the techniques I use most often is an Interaction Cost Analysis (ICA). This is a particularly good tool because it can be used with simple estimations *at any point in the process,* even as early as a wireframe or whiteboard sketch. With practice, it can be done very quickly. In addition, it's possible to go beyond estimations and use this to get more precise results, which makes it one of the most flexible tools on this list.

As mentioned, an ICA can be used either in a structured way (to validate) or a more relaxed way (to estimate). I find that it's most valuable as an estimation, which I'll cover in detail here, but I'll also give you pointers on how you can use it in a more structured way in the section "How to measure effort more precisely with an ICA."

This is not a new technique, but it isn't used as often as it should be. In its place, we typically see folks simply counting the number of steps, screens, or clicks in a process. While this can be helpful, it fails to account for *the amount of effort in each step.* Certainly, a small target positioned far away is harder to interact with than a large target sitting nearby; different interactions require different amounts of effort.

Instead, an ICA measures both *the number of steps* and *the relative effort inside them.* To demonstrate, let's look at workflows from two print design apps. One of these apps provides accelerators for common interactions, while the other does not.

Write out the process step-by-step

As with any technique mentioned in this chapter, when you want to compare interfaces, your best bet is to evaluate the process of completing one or more specific tasks. The more tasks you compare, the more complete your picture will be.

For this example, because these tools are both used for desktop publishing, we'll look at completing a task that involves drawing a text box, pasting text into it, repositioning page elements, and editing text.

We'll start by writing out the MEP (Most Ergonomic Path) in each tool:

INTERFACE A	INTERFACE B
1. Go to Rectangle Text Box tool	1. Type T to switch to the Type tool
2. Drag to draw a text box where desired	2. Drag to draw a text box where desired
3. Type CMD+V to paste text in to the text box	3. Type CMD+V to paste text in to the text box
4. Go click the item tool	4. Type Esc to switch to the selection tool
5. Drag to select items	5. Drag to select items
6. Drag to reposition items	6. Drag to reposition items
7. Go click the content tool	7. Double-click the text box to place the text cursor
8. Click to place the text cursor	

For workflows that often get repeated, I recommend including several repetitions here.

Estimate the effort required

Once you've made this list, do a gut check on the level of effort each interaction will require *relative to all the other interactions* you're comparing. For each step, ask yourself, "If I knew exactly what to do, what is the minimum effort needed to actually *do it*?" and then indicate the amount of effort as either Small, Medium, or Large. Let's do that here:

INTERFACE A		INTERFACE B	
1. Go to Rectangle Text Box tool	Lrg	1. Type T to switch to the Type tool	Med
2. Drag to draw a text box where desired	Sml	2. Drag to draw a text box where desired	Sml
3. Type CMD+V to paste text in to the text box	Med	3. Type CMD+V to paste text in to the text box	Med
4. Go click the item tool	Lrg	4. Type Esc to switch to the selection tool	Med
5. Drag to select items	Sml	5. Drag to select items	Sml
6. Drag to reposition items	Sml	6. Drag to reposition items	Sml
7. Go click the content tool	Lrg	7. Double-click the text box to place the text cursor	Sml
8. Click to place the text cursor	Sml		

If you're having difficulty deciding which step is more ergonomic, ask yourself which one could be done more quickly five times in a row. It's not perfect, but it's often a good proxy—we'll cover this process in more detail with Technique 2, up ahead.

While we're only making estimates here, with practice, it's usually not difficult to do this well. Right away, you might notice that *Interface A* requires more steps, and the steps are more difficult, on average. Most times, like in this case, the difference in ergonomic effort between a set of options isn't tiny; an estimation can usually help you find the winner.

While the total number of steps doesn't fully account for the ergonomic effort in a workflow, the shorter process is often the easiest, provided there's not a notable difference in the ergonomic effort required in each step. (An example of this would be a two-step process requiring small, fiddly buttons, compared to a process broken into three or more steps where every step was much easier.) In this case, it's clear-cut: *Interface B* offers both a shorter process and an easier process, ergonomically. *Interface A* required steps that were substantially more difficult, on average, so even if we could eliminate a step to simplify this process, it would still require more ergonomic effort overall.

Compare results and draw conclusions

It's usually easy to spot a winner. But if you need more clarity, a simple technique is to measure the differences in the number of steps *per effort level* between the two interfaces.

1. Start by counting the number of Small-, Medium-, and Large-effort steps in each interface.

2. Next, write down which interface requires more steps for a given effort level and by how many.

For example, for this task, *Interface A* required one Medium-effort step, while *Interface B* required three. In this case, we'd write "+2 for *Interface B*" to indicate that it required two more Medium-effort steps than the other option.

	INTERFACE A	INTERFACE B	DIFFERENCE
Small-effort	4 steps	4 steps	Tied
Medium-effort	1 step	3 steps	+2 for Interface B
Large-effort	3 steps	0 steps	+3 for Interface A

This makes it easy to form a concise summary of these differences:

> *To complete this task,* Interface B *required two more Medium-effort steps than* Interface A, *while* Interface A *required three more Large-effort steps. We conclude that* Interface B *is the more ergonomic option for this task overall.*

With a summary like this, it's often plainly evident which option is the winner. It can be valuable to include this kind of summary when sharing your findings with others.

How to measure effort more precisely with an ICA

With practice, simple estimates can be effective when doing an ICA, and are good enough for comparing most interfaces. But experience matters here, as estimates made by less experienced designers can vary quite a bit—by as much as 70%[1]. If you're new to this, you're not out of luck: try pairing up with someone more experienced or put the question to your team to get a broader consensus.

In closing, I can't neglect to mention another option for getting more predictable results. However, I'd currently advise against using it in most cases. Several effort models (such as GOMS, KLM, and ACT-R) provide guidance on the effort required to complete a set of actions. These models can be used to calculate effort manually or, more commonly, by leveraging tools that utilize these frameworks. In my experience, setting this up can be a bit cumbersome, but as new and better tools for this pop up from time to time, a modern tool that leverages one of these effort models may be available by the time you read this.[2]

1. "Reducing the Variability between Novice Modelers: Results of a Tool for Human Performance Modeling Produced through Human-Centered Design" John, Bonnie E. http://acs.ist.psu.edu/papers/brims2010/10-BRIMS-119%20John.pdf Retrieved Jan 26, 2021

2. Interestingly, it's also technically possible to automate this process. Researchers have explored a system that can automatically analyze the UI, map the different paths a user can take throughout an app or interface, and create scores for different ways of completing tasks. This is very exciting, as it could be used to perform a sort of "ergonomic regression testing" to monitor for ergonomic setbacks, akin to what software engineers use to ensure no new bugs arise and accidentally get released to users. This would provide an automated way to watch for changes to your ergonomic effort baseline as a safeguard. Unfortunately, no such tool is available for public use at the time of writing. I'm hopeful that will change.

Summary of Technique 1: Interaction Cost Analysis (ICA)

One of the biggest advantages of doing an Interaction Cost Analysis (ICA) is that it's possible to do at any point in the process, with very little investment. I recommend doing it at the start of the process, with estimates and early-stage wireframes, and as a periodic gut-check throughout the design process.

Remember that counting clicks doesn't tell you the whole story, so if you hear a teammate counting, it's a good reminder to use an ICA instead.

TECHNIQUE 2

Speed Running

Next up is speed running. If you're not familiar with it, this term comes from the world of video gaming. It's a race where, after a lot of practice, players will try to reach a particular goal in as little time as possible.

When these players hurry through a game, there are inevitably trickier parts that slow them down. The added pressure of trying to hurry can make these tricky areas stand out and become more apparent. We can use that to our advantage.

We'll use speed running to race through different methods of completing a task. Unlike an ICA, this can only be done after first building the actual interface or (at a minimum) a suitably detailed prototype. On the plus side, however, you can often get great results with or without real users.

Oh, and did I mention *it's fun*?

Select the tasks you will test

As always, start by identifying which methods of completing a task you want to test. Just as with other techniques, I've found it's often easiest to get good results when there's a repeating element to the task (e.g., "Create five text boxes, with each one containing a different paragraph of text from this document") since it can help make differences more apparent.

Find the people with the most experience (hint: this might be you)

You'll want to test the interface with someone who knows it well—the more experience they have with it, the better. This means that, for an all-new interface, the person who knows it best is typically someone *on your team*. Don't be shy about doing these tests on your own, either, as your goal is to measure the issues that persist even when a person knows the process well—this is not a learnability test, after all.

For interfaces that are already in use, though, it's common for your most experienced users to know it better than you do. This means that when redesigning an interface, it's valuable to do testing in two stages. First, run the tests with yourself or someone on your team. If the new interface passes the test, validate your results by doing a second round of testing with a user who has a lot of experience completing the task in the current interface.

When testing with your users, you must be careful. Even when working with your most experienced users, it can be easy to underestimate how long it will take them to get up to speed with the new version. For the best results, you'll want them to develop a muscle-memory for the new interface, so the better they can internalize the new workflow, the better your results will be. I usually take a few minutes to train them on the updated interface, answer any questions they may have, and then give them *as much time as possible* to explore and rehearse before we start the test. Always let them do a few trial runs to get up to speed and uncover knowledge gaps. Remember, we're trying to recreate the experience of someone who knows the process *intimately*, so the more practice they can get in, the better.

And...go!

To run the test, I recommend starting with the newer, redesigned interface and then moving on to the previous interface for the second half—for whatever reason, doing things in this order tends to make it easier to feel whether the original or redesigned interface was more comfortable (i.e., "Does the old interface feel like an old friend, or just old and busted?").

Get a stopwatch ready. Give the speed runner a countdown, then time how long it takes them to reach the end. Let them try as many times as they like—*they're* not being tested; *the interface* is. Ultimately, you'll keep the fastest time. Do the same thing with the other interface and keep the fastest time here, too.

There will often be a clear winner. If not, increase the number of repetitions (e.g., instead of doing the process with five text boxes, do it with ten) to help make the difference more apparent.

If they make mistakes here, that's OK, so long as they're caused by ergonomic effort and not by gaps in knowledge. I like to ask, "Would they still make this mistake if they knew the interface better?" If not, give them a little time to get more familiar. Try to let them keep going until there are no knowledge-based errors—the only thing we want to slow them down is ergonomic effort.

Compare results and draw conclusions

Ultimately, you'll compare the time it takes to complete the task in one interface versus another. This makes picking a winner very straightforward; shorter times are better. After you get results, ask yourself, "Is there any way this could be done in half the time?" By posing a bold question like this, it can help you to reframe your thinking to center around more impactful changes you can make.

In addition, after running each test, it's valuable to ask the speed runner about their experience. I like to ask, "What got in your way the most during your run?" There will usually be one or more specific points of friction that stand out to them. Take special note of these, as these bottlenecks are prime candidates for making improvements.

Bonus tip: Play it back in slow motion

If you want to fine-tune an interaction, watch it in slow motion. Watching a slow-motion video of someone using an interface can help you feel what skilled users feel when trying to fly through a process. There's an aching desire to *just get on with it already.* Make a video or screen recording of someone racing through an interaction and play it back at one-quarter or one-eighth speed, and then ask yourself what caused the process to take as long as it did (and what can be done about it).

This is especially valuable to do with high-use interactions (see Chapter 2).

Summary of Technique 2: Speed Running

Speed running is a great way to get a clearer answer about which interface requires less ergonomic effort and can help you to identify your biggest pain points. It requires either a fully built interface or a highly detailed prototype to run this kind of test, but it provides excellent results, and people tend to have a great time doing it.

TECHNIQUE 3

"Extended" Usability Testing

As you've seen, "first-look" usability testing only offers users a few minutes to give their first impressions, which makes it best suited for uncovering issues with learnability. Instead, when testing for ergonomics, I like to do an "extended" type of testing on more significant interface changes whenever time permits.

Compared to "first-look" testing, this "extended" variety gives users longer to kick the tires. It involves providing experienced users with a fully built interface and giving them a week or more to play with it. You can think of it as a focused form of beta testing with some additional structure and an emphasis on education. While this requires more time and effort than other techniques mentioned here, it can provide some of the best insights and can be combined with "first-look" testing to reduce these overheads.

A word of warning, though. Because this involves setting up a group of users with a new interface, I recommend *only* running this test if you can switch users back and forth between the current and proposed interface with relative ease. The last thing you want is to switch someone over, discover a huge bug, and then be unable to switch them back immediately. Otherwise, you're better served by the techniques described earlier.

Bug hunting comes first

Speaking of bugs, do what you can to eliminate them in the workflows being tested. Most beta testing is also bug hunting, but bugs can get in the way of an otherwise ergonomic workflow. If you have time, you should perform a short internal beta or bug bash focused on the workflows being tested to iron out issues *before* doing this "extended" testing.

Piggyback on "first-look" usability testing

Doing this "extended" testing alongside typical "first-look" testing can streamline the process. So as you recruit participants, be sure to include folks who are highly experienced with the parts of the app you'll be testing. A great way to find suitable candidates is by providing an in-app feature where users can opt in to give feedback on upcoming changes. For best results, be sure you only make this option visible to users who have accumulated a lot of time completing the tasks in question.

To check for a suitable experience level, I recommend asking users what issues they *actively* face when completing these tasks with the current interface. If they say anything about things being hard to figure out or difficult for them to remember, they may not be out of the learning phase yet. In this case, they may not be a good candidate for the "extended" portion of this test.

You'll be moving this "extended" test group over to the redesigned interface for the duration of the test—I recommend a week or two—so be sure to confirm that they are comfortable with this ahead of time.

In the end, you'll have two groups of users: the regular "first-look" testing group and the highly experienced "extended" testing group. When the time comes, run the "first-look" testing with the non-expert group as you normally would. But for the highly experienced group, you'll go through the process of documenting what they do today, getting their first impressions of the new interface, providing them with an in-depth walkthrough, and coming back to check on it 1–2 weeks later:

1. **To start, have them demonstrate the process of completing these tasks using the interface they already know well.** Make a recording for reference later, if possible. Take a moment to make a note of any issues they face, as users in this group are more likely to have issues that are ergonomic in nature.

2. **Introduce them to the redesigned interface.** At this point, it's good to do traditional "first-look" testing with this highly experienced group. Because you already need to introduce them to this new interface to do this "extended" testing, you have an opportunity to get their initial impressions at this point.

3. **Confirm that they're still comfortable using this new interface exclusively for the rest of the test.** Users may need to back out for any number of reasons. If they're still game, set them up with the redesigned interface in place of the interface they normally use.

4. **Get them through the learning phase as quickly as possible.** Give them a thorough education and encourage them to use the interface as much as they can over the duration of the test. Urge them to reach out with questions they uncover. Getting out of the learning phase often takes more than a week in the real world, so we want to accelerate the process as much as possible.

5. **After a week or more, do a follow-up with these users.** Get a recording of them completing these tasks with the new interface as they give you their feedback on it. If they encounter issues with learnability or software bugs, note them, but remember that your current focus is on ergonomic effort.

6. **Switch them back to the old interface again.** Ask for their reaction—as they compare things out loud, it's common to hear complaints about the redesigned interface, so take special note of these.

At the end of the conversation, users will often ask whether they can keep using the redesigned interface—if they do, that's clearly a great sign.

Compare results and draw conclusions

After doing this testing, it's common to see patterns emerge, even with a small group of users. This makes it straightforward to spot issues and identify improvements.

Additionally, the "before and after" screen recordings you made can help you narrow in on key issues and demonstrate them to stakeholders, as needed.

Summary of Technique 3: "Extended" Usability Testing

By doing this alongside "first-look" usability testing, you can evaluate more than just learnability. Doing both tests together saves time and effort while providing a more comprehensive look at the overall effort required.

Ultimately, this takes longer than other techniques in this chapter but can provide some of the clearest insights.

KEY POINTS TO REMEMBER

Chapter 1 highlighted how traditional "first-look" usability testing tends to overlook ergonomic issues. But because it's better to catch these pain points ahead of your users, and because it's vital to ensure that the ergonomic effort baseline doesn't increase from one version to the next, it's wise to measure this effort.

Uncovering this friction doesn't have to be laborious or difficult. In short, there are options available that are quick, fun, and can be combined with other testing you're already doing. Each has different strengths, so use the techniques here in different scenarios depending on your available time and where you are in the design process.

TRY THIS

- When you're working on a new interface, do an Interaction Cost Analysis (ICA) as soon as you have an idea of the direction you're thinking of going in. Use this technique throughout the design process, as you make changes, as a form of spot-checking. With practice, you can do this in your head when reviewing work during design crit with teammates, as well.

- Do speed running as soon as you can get good results, which is typically right after the interface (or a good prototype) has been built. It's fun—lean into that by holding carefree contests. Award a prize for the fastest time in each interface. Test it with your team members and connect with experienced users to get them involved.

- Use "extended" usability testing to get a more thorough evaluation of a near-final interface before it goes live for everyone. It takes the most time, but this often provides the clearest picture of the ergonomic friction in your interface out of the techniques mentioned here.

- When comparing your product to a competitor, ask yourself, "Was that only hard because I had to figure it out?" I'll ask myself this repeatedly as I go through this process, because it's *so easy* to conflate the two types of effort. You will inherently be much more familiar with your own product, which means there's a higher chance that you'll experience learning effort while looking at your competitors' products. Try to focus purely on ergonomics.

UP NEXT

These three techniques help you to spot ergonomic issues. Next, we'll look at how to spot ergonomic *improvements* using the CUPID System. With it, you'll find these improvements proactively during the design phase, saving you time and reducing user pain. ⊙→

PART II

5

THE CUPID SYSTEM:
A FIVE-STEP CHECKLIST
FOR IMPROVING
LONG-TERM USABILITY
IN ADVANCE

We've covered a lot of ground, so let's quickly recap what we've discussed so far:

- **In Chapter 1, we saw how splitting usability into *two types of effort* helps us keep an eye on the permanent day-to-day effort of using an app.** As we're defining it, learning effort accounts for any source of friction a user can reduce by getting more familiar. By contrast, ergonomic effort is every source of effort they cannot. This framework gives us tools that enable us to make smarter decisions about what we design and build.

- **In Chapter 2, we saw how users start to care less about learning effort and more about ergonomic effort as their experience grows.** Because this is important (and not always obvious), we explored how this can be communicated visually with your team and stakeholders. Additionally, we've seen how making ergonomic improvements to more common tasks helps us to reduce the ongoing effort faced by every user.

- **In Chapter 3, we discussed how the amount of ergonomic effort required to use your app becomes a line you must not cross.** An ergonomic effort baseline forms the root of an "unspoken contract" with your users. From version to version, any setbacks here—even small ones—can cause disappointment and outrage. It's vital to make sure that ergonomic effort stays the same or gets better from one version to the next.

- **Lastly, in Chapter 4, we looked at several ways to evaluate how much ergonomic effort exists in an interface.** This helps you ensure that you're effectively reducing this effort throughout the design process.

Up until now, we've explored the importance of ergonomic effort in keeping users happy in the long term, along with some tools for keeping a close eye on it.

Now, we'll shift gears to focus entirely on specific things you can do to decrease this effort. In each of the remaining chapters, you'll find examples of how to improve the ergonomics of an interface across five major categories.

How to improve long-term ease of use proactively

While learnability rightly gets a lot of design attention and is routinely addressed with targeted improvements, there seems to be an absence of any focused techniques for improving ergonomics, specifically.

Instead, these kinds of improvements typically get made in a more ad hoc way. After a product has been built and ergonomic friction starts getting noticed by users, software teams often start hearing complaints:

"Users keep saying that this button is too small."

"OK, we'll add it to the backlog."

But this is *reactive*, not *proactive*, which means that only the biggest issues get any attention, and improvements often only get made *after* users have felt the pain of them.

Think about that for a moment. For this kind of design process to work, it depends on users feeling pain.

That's clearly not ideal. Worse, you won't always know just how bad it is until later. We've discussed how issues like these are often hidden by learning effort at the start, and how setbacks to an ergonomic baseline can greatly frustrate your users. In other words, one of the most important things designers need to keep an eye on *often remains hidden until it's too late.*

Seeing how valuable it would be to make these kinds of improvements proactively, I looked for a reliable way to reduce these issues while still in the design phase.

To do this, I kept detailed notes about all the places I noticed ergonomic effort for seven years. Patterns began to emerge, and I was able to group this effort into a set of five categories. To remember them more easily, I gave the categories a five-letter acronym: C-U-P-I-D.

These categories are places where ergonomic improvements can be found. For each of these "CUPID principles," I captured an overarching theme:

CUPID PRINCIPLE	THEME
Clear	Be discernible quickly.
Unobstructed	Get out of the way.
Predictable	Make it possible to anticipate things.
Indulgent	Accept sloppier input.
Digestible	Reduce mental strain.

In general, interfaces tend to require less ergonomic effort when they are more *Clear*, *Unobstructed*, *Predictable*, *Indulgent*, and *Digestible*. We'll explore each of these in detail in the following chapters.

These principles form the backbone of what I call the CUPID System. As this provides a map of where ergonomic friction is often found in an interface, this gives us a way to go through and address this effort systematically, leaving no stone unturned.

This friction doesn't always fit neatly into a single category, but that's OK. For our purposes, it's less important which category we find friction in and more important *that the friction gets found and addressed.*

The CUPID System in use

I've found the CUPID System to be valuable while working independently and with a larger group during design crit. There are advantages to each, as we'll explore ahead.

How to use the CUPID System on your own

At the start of a project, when you have an initial wireframe or whiteboard sketch, use this system to perform a spot-check to find issues and improvements you may not have already caught.

I recommend going through each of these CUPID principles one at a time for the best results. Think of this as a sort of preflight checklist; when you go through this process methodically, it helps ensure you're not overlooking anything. To do this, start by asking "How might we"-style questions, using both the principle and its theme:

> *"How can this be made more Clear? What more can we do to be discernible quickly?"*

When you use this system, some answers might present themselves right away. But the biggest value often comes from digging deeper, as there are many applications that are less obvious. So to make this easier, this book includes a list of specific objectives and tactics for each principle. These can help you uncover issues lurking just below the surface, so it's helpful to reference them as you go.

Appendix C contains a list of these principles, themes, objectives, and tactics at the end of this book, and the next five chapters include examples for each. These will make more sense when we get to them, but to give you an example, here are the objectives for *Clear*:

- Make the state of the app more apparent.
- Give obvious and timely feedback.
- Provide a distinct sense of context.

As before, ask yourself "How might we"-style questions to dig into each of these:

> *"What more can we do to give obvious and timely feedback?"*

Take your time, and be as thorough as possible before moving on to the next principle. Repeat this process for each of the CUPID principles.

While you can use this system throughout the design process, it's often most valuable to do this at the start of the project and again right before taking it to design crit for feedback from your team.

Speaking of which…

How to use the CUPID System with your team during design crit

When reviewing work with a design team, I've found this system to be helpful in a couple of different ways.

First, it's a great tool to use when reviewing your teammates' work. With enough practice, you can do this exercise in your head to spot issues and improvements that the group may otherwise overlook. (It's the secret weapon I use to catch things that are often missed.)

But it can also be valuable to work together with your design team to go through this process as a group. This is most helpful for bigger projects that can benefit from more scrutiny.

Like with "first-look" usability testing, many of your teammates will see an interface for the first time when reviewing it during design crit. Because of this, issues with learnability are often top of mind. This makes the CUPID System valuable for helping the group look beyond first impressions.

To conduct this exercise with your team, start by putting the CUPID principles across the top of a whiteboard, virtual canvas, or spread-sheet as column headers. Then, as a group, go through the exercise together, one principle at a time, asking the same "How might we"-style questions:

> *"OK, we've gone through* Clear *and* Unobstructed, *so let's move on to* Predictable. *What more can we do to* make it possible to anticipate things? *How might we* create stable targets, make inputs more consistent, *or* produce dependable outcomes?*"

Using each principle as a column header, write out the suggestions from the group.

C	U	P	I	D
Clear	Unobstructed	Predictable	Indulgent	Digestible

To use this system with a group, write the principles as headers and collect suggestions from the group underneath.

Move together as a group, focusing on one principle at a time, to allow folks to properly step into the necessary headspace. As ergonomic effort can be elusive, this focused approach helps the group do a better job of spotting friction that may be tucked away. During this process, folks will inevitably stumble across fixes in categories other than the current one. That's not a bad thing, but I recommend asking them to kindly hang on to these suggestions until you arrive at that category together. At the end, after giving each of the principles your undivided attention individually, you can open up the floor to collect any of these remaining suggestions.

Because most people are new to this process and these principles, I recommend making a list of the principles, themes, objectives, and tactics available to everyone in the group. This can be done with "CUPID Cheat Sheet" handouts or by presenting a similar graphic onscreen as you go through each principle.

For example, the Cheat Sheet for the letter C contains:

Clear

How might we be discernible quickly?

1. *Make the state of the app more apparent*
2. *Give obvious and timely feedback*
3. *Provide a distinct sense of context*

As a reminder, you can find CUPID Cheat Sheets for all five of these principles at the end of this book, in Appendix C. These are included just before the back cover for your (ergonomic) convenience as a quick reference.

Meet "Morgan"

Let's explore how we can use the CUPID System to help improve an interface. In the remaining chapters, we'll go through these principles one at a time as we imagine the process of refining an app. While the interface we will review is fictitious, the goal is to give you a sense of what it's like to use this system in practice on an actual project.

To do this, let's imagine a professional tool used by someone as part of their job as an example of an interface with a heavier use case. Our imaginary user—let's call them "Morgan"—works at a milk tea stand and uses a register to enter order details for each customer. To set the scene, imagine this shop is located near a train station, with big groups of customers arriving in waves. Try to imagine Morgan's urgency when they have a long line of customers all hurrying to get their orders before their trains depart.

The register interface we'll examine is a tool Morgan uses daily for work, so they have a lot of experience with it. Keep this in mind and pay attention to how the issues they face aren't due to gaps in knowledge. No amount of learning the interface better will help them move any more smoothly, as the friction they're facing is baked into the interactions themselves. In the same vein, note how very few of these improvements (if any) will make the interface substantially easier to learn. The main improvement will be to the amount of *ergonomic* effort present in the interface.

For the sake of clarity

Some of the examples in the upcoming chapters may seem obvious. However, keep in mind that ergonomic friction will often appear in far subtler ways. In other words, these examples are included in this book because they more clearly illustrate the root of the problem. But in the real world, individual issues can be far sneakier, so going through this process slowly and methodically is especially important.

In the upcoming chapters, these examples are organized into objectives and tactics. These categories each have broader implications that are far more helpful to remember than any individual example. I'll provide some guidance on these broader elements as we go.

Lastly, I should note that the fixes shown here aren't meant to be "perfect solutions". So, while better options may be available, remember that the goal is to showcase a wide variety of improvement areas rather than teach you how to create the perfect register interface.

KEY POINTS TO REMEMBER

The CUPID System is a tool to help you more easily fix issues with ergonomics well before users feel this pain themselves. It can be used both while you're designing on your own and as a group activity with other members of your team. With practice, it can help you to spot many more improvements than you might otherwise.

TRY THIS

- **Learn how to use the CUPID System.** Go through each CUPID principle, one at a time, and ask, "How could this be made more (*Clear, Unobstructed, Predictable, Indulgent,* or *Digestible*)?" Use each principle's theme to help center your focus on each category (e.g., when looking for ways to be more Clear, ask how you can "Be discernible quickly"). Take this further by going through the list of objectives and tactics for each principle to uncover less obvious issues.

- **Use the CUPID System on your own.** Use it as a spot-check, starting with the earliest wireframes at the start of a design project or as a final check to ensure things are in order before bringing it to design crit.

- **To get help from your team, use the CUPID System during design crit.** Write out the principles as headers (once your team is more familiar, you can shorten this to the letters C-U-P-I-D). Make CUPID Cheat Sheets available containing the principles, themes, objectives, and tactics. Get feedback for one principle at a time before moving on to the next. After you've gone through every principle individually, open the floor to collect any remaining fixes that may have been spotted along the way.

- **Try it for yourself.** You don't have to take my word for it. Start by taking an interface to design crit for feedback as you normally would. Afterward, review the interface again on your own using the CUPID System. With a little practice, you'll likely be surprised by how many more issues this helps you to avoid.

UP NEXT

In the remaining chapters, we'll look at many examples of how to use the CUPID System to make an interface easier to use in the long run.

We'll kick off our tour by looking at how to make interfaces that communicate more clearly with users. ➔

6

C FOR CLEAR:

HOW TO DESIGN
INTERFACES SO THAT
USERS ARE NEVER
MISTAKEN

I was once put in charge of redesigning an interface that I was told some users were having difficulties with. As I spoke with users directly, I discovered many of their issues stemmed from the use of a single color. This color—a shade of lime green—provided such poor color contrast that even users with good vision had difficulty making it out against a white or gray background.

Importantly, these users *knew* what they were looking for, but it was inherently tricky even with this knowledge. As with all the ergonomic improvements we're about to see, it's not enough that users can figure out what to do. We also need to ensure we don't get in the way of their ability to do it.

Being able to move through an interface quickly and with confidence often depends on a user's ability to answer split-second questions about it:

> *"Where is the item I'm looking for?"*
>
> *"Which item is currently selected?"*
>
> *"Was my input received?"*

A clear interface ensures that users are *never mistaken* about these kinds of things. It allows them to move more quickly while making fewer errors than they would otherwise. The faster this information can be received and understood, the less time and effort will be wasted. As a result, our bar for quality shouldn't be whether it's comprehensible, but rather whether it is *unmistakable*.

As a reminder, these remaining five chapters will look at an interface used by Morgan, an (imaginary) employee at a milk tea stand near a busy train station. It's the interface for the register they use each day, and it has many ergonomic issues. Ahead, we'll look at ways to redesign this interface to demonstrate how better UI Ergonomics can make their daily use much more efficient and comfortable.

C.U.P.I.D.

Clear: how might we be discernible quickly?

1. Make the state of the app more apparent
2. Give obvious and timely feedback
3. Provide a distinct sense of context

Make the state of the app more apparent

When Morgan was opening for business every morning, they needed to switch on the register and sign into their account. This is because a partner delivery service was connected to this device and required a user to be signed in before the shop appeared to customers as "open" and available to take orders that day.

This meant that each day, Morgan needed to sign in *as soon as possible* so that they didn't miss any of the morning rush.

Unfortunately, the register device took several minutes to start up and sync with the database, and the amount of time this took changed dramatically each day—anywhere from 2 minutes to 20 minutes. Worse, the only indication that it was ready was that the words "Sign in" appeared on a button label when it had finished. As a result, every day, Morgan would have to keep checking on the device to see if it was ready, and this slowed them down as they performed their other start-of-day tasks.

When the system was starting up, it would show a small progress indicator...

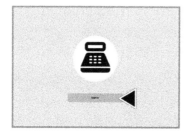

...and when it was finished, it would show a sign in button.

These states looked so similar that it made it harder to know if it was ready at a glance, which slowed Morgan down as they opened up shop in the morning.

This can be made much clearer. First, let's make the loading and completed states visually distinct from each other. This will make it easier to determine at a glance when things have finished loading, even from a distance.

To take this further, we'll allow Morgan to choose a sound to play as well, if they'd like, and give them the ability to have a notification sent to the device they have with them.

These changes will make it easier for Morgan to know when the system is ready for them, even when they're not immediately in front of the device. As a result, Morgan can focus their entire attention on other tasks without fear of missing their cue to take action.

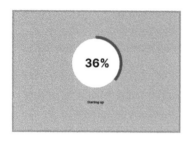

Instead, we can make it plainly obvious when the system is starting up...

...as well as make it visually distinct when the system is ready to go.

Now that Morgan can clearly see this from a distance, they can spend less of their effort monitoring it as they open shop.

How to make the state of the app more apparent

Ensure that users can tell if the system is ready.

[See the previous example story]

Make modes more obvious.

When a mode can be activated so that inputs are interpreted by the system differently, users need to be able to immediately tell when they are or are not in this mode. Use a strong visual indicator when in a different mode and consider leveraging other helpful forms of feedback (like audio and haptics).

Give a clear indication of which item will be acted on.

Provide distinct selection states in graphical interfaces and clearly disambiguate when using voice interfaces. Ensure that visual selection indicators are obvious and only appear for one item or group at a time. For voice interfaces, provide ways to ask for clarification.

Give users a clear sense of progress.

Knowing that progress is being made—and that the end is getting closer—helps users gain more confidence that their effort is being transformed into meaningful work. Also, it gives them a better understanding of when things will be completed. Show users how far along they are in a process or set whenever possible.

Give obvious and timely feedback

Whenever a customer wanted to order a particular item, Morgan would need to tap to select it on their screen. Selecting an item would open a details page, which would appear a moment or two later.

Unfortunately, this was their only indication that they had tapped it correctly. There was no other form of feedback if it was successfully tapped, which made it hard for Morgan to know whether they'd properly tapped the right area until a moment had passed.

When Morgan tapped the screen...

...a moment would go by before there was any visual indication.

This often left them stuck in a moment of awkwardness from not knowing if they'd aimed poorly or if the system was slow.

Momentary delays can feel like an eternity when a long line of customers is waiting, and it can be frustrating if it turns out the target was missed.

Let's change this. While it would be best to eliminate the delay entirely, there are things we can do to help even if that's not an option.

In our redesigned interface, we'll provide strong and immediate visual feedback by changing the appearance of an item's border the moment it is tapped. We'll also provide the option of hearing customizable audio cues to distinguish whether a tap was on or off target. This way, it's easier for Morgan to recover from a missed tap (which is especially common when working quickly). Doing so ensures that there will no longer be momentary confusion slowing things down and causing frustration again and again throughout the day.

Users can pick up on signals in as little as 50–200ms, with this time getting closer to 50ms as they gain experience.[1] Delays longer than this can break a user's sense that they're interacting with the UI directly, and longer delays can break a user's flow or even their concentration. If a delay of over 10 seconds is unavoidable, we would want to show a progress meter (ideally) or another kind of loading indicator as soon as possible.

---

1. Card, S. K., Moran, T. P., & Newell, A. (Eds.). (1986). The psychology of human-computer interaction. Mahwah, NJ: Lawrence Erlbaum Associates.

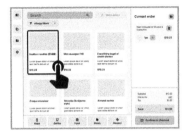

To improve this, we can add instant feedback within 50ms of a tap...

...which gives Morgan reassurance that they'd aimed correctly.

This helps Morgan to both correct errors and prepare for next steps more easily. This feedback clears up confusion.

How to give obvious and timely feedback

Give feedback as quickly as you can.

[See the previous example story]

Be sure to send the right message.

Ambiguous signals—like a blinking light—can be hard to figure out when they are used to indicate different things under different circumstances. Instead, aim to make the feedback you provide *completely* unmistakable. This is highly dependent on context, so take a moment to ask yourself how something might be misinterpreted given what you know about your users and how they'll use the interface. Chances are there's a clearer way of communicating.

Leverage signal strength to make feedback clearer.

Feedback only helps users as soon as they're able to process it. Stronger signals, like more drastic changes in contrast, more intense haptic vibration, and louder audio get processed by the brain more quickly,[2] so leverage this by degrees to make the important things stand out. Use the most attention-grabbing techniques when speed is essential, and be careful not to overwhelm users when things are less urgent.

Use previews as a form of advance feedback.

Previews help users move even more quickly by providing feedback *before* they act, which can help them avoid bad outcomes. Specifically, give users previews whenever an action takes a lot of trial and error to perform correctly (or if it will be costly to undo).

---

2. Card, et al.

Provide a distinct sense of context

Throughout the day, as Morgan helped customers in person, customers elsewhere would place advance orders for pickup. This was communicated in the UI through a small indicator dot that appeared on the *Order Queue* tab whenever there were pending orders waiting.

Missing an order in this queue meant that a customer might arrive before their order was ready, which would make them unhappy and require Morgan to drop everything to rush to prepare their order right then and there.

Unfortunately, this happened a lot—because the indicator dot on the *Order Queue* tab was so hard to see, Morgan had to spend extra effort checking this tab periodically to catch any orders that may have snuck in while their attention was on other things. This became a common source of distraction and caused a lot of additional overhead—not to mention awkward encounters with customers.

Whenever there were new orders in the queue, a pale dot would appear in the upper right.

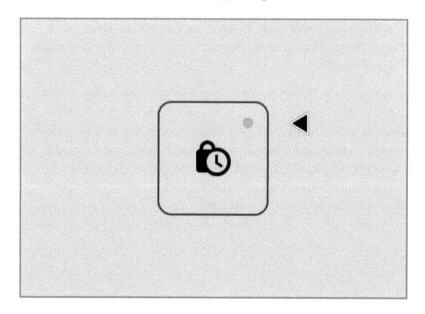

This indicator was hard to see, so even though Morgan knew what to look for, it took effort to keep an eye on it.

Thankfully, we can make this *much* easier to discern. When new orders are in the queue, we can have the tab appear with a thick, high-contrast outline and a prominent badge showing the number of pending orders.

In addition, we can allow Morgan to have the border of the screen flash when a new order arrives as well. All of this helps to ensure they would never have any doubts about whether there were orders that needed attention.

This gives them the context they need at a glance.

Instead, by making this indicator more obvious, we've reduced the overall effort for a common interaction.

How to provide a distinct sense of context

Use easily discernible structure and indicators.

[See the previous example story]

Ensure that users know where they are, what's ahead, and how to get back.

When users can quickly determine where they are in an interface—which screen they're on, where they are in a process, and how to get where they want next—it gives them a better sense of control. It also makes it easier for them to move more confidently when they know they can always return to where they started without much fuss. Mark pages plainly, lean into clear navigation, and always provide a clear escape route back to home base.

KEY POINTS TO REMEMBER

A clear interface can leave users feeling like they're in control. When things are clear to a user, they are better informed, which allows them to quickly make better decisions about what to do next.

UP NEXT

Even when users feel like they're in control, they can't take action if the interface won't let them. Ahead, we'll look at how obstructions can get in the way of users being able to move as quickly as they'd like, and what to do when delays and interruptions can't be avoided completely. →

7

U FOR UNOBSTRUCTED:
HOW TO DESIGN
INTERFACES THAT
STAY OUT OF THE WAY
OF USERS

Interfaces can create obstacles. This was on full display as I ran to catch a flight with a friend. While we hurried through the airport, she dragged her luggage along with one hand as she hunted through her phone with her other hand. Because one of her hands was occupied with her luggage, she only had a single hand free to operate her device, which made it harder to reach certain controls. The app she was using required her to dig through a series of menus to get to the information she needed. She was in a hurry, and the interface kept getting *in her way*.

There are several ways that an interface can put obstacles in someone's path, from a disregard for the limitations of human body movement, to long and complex processes, to stutters and delays of all kinds. Ahead, we'll look at some ways to reduce these obstructions to let users move as freely as possible.

C.U.P.I.D.

Unobstructed: how might we get out of the way?

1. Reduce unnecessary delays
2. Improve speed and comfort during unavoidable delays
3. Work with human movement
4. Make direct paths

Reduce unnecessary delays

Whenever Morgan completed a transaction, the register would display a message saying, "Please wait—receipt is printing." This message would remain front and center in a modal until the receipt had finished printing, and while it was displayed, the system would not accept any other input. If that wasn't frustrating enough, after the receipt had printed, the modal would slowly fade out over several moments. As it faded away, it prevented further inputs from being made until it had disappeared entirely.

This happened after *every* transaction. Each time it happened, Morgan, the customer, and the next customer in line would all have to wait awkwardly for the printer to finish and the message to disappear before they could move on to the next order. The interface was standing in their way.

When a transaction was completed, the register would print a receipt.

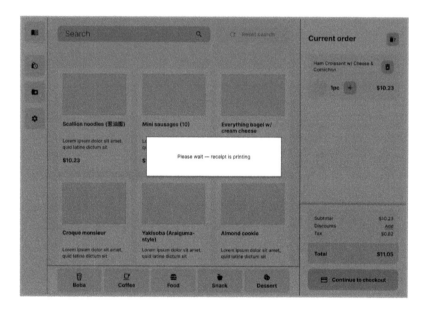

But because it would display a message while the receipt printed, Morgan was unable to start with the next customer until it was done.

The words "Please wait" should raise all kinds of red flags for interface designers.

Thankfully, there was no technical limitation that required this delay to exist. In this case, the system was otherwise capable of taking the next order, but Morgan was being blocked due to the way the modal was designed. Things would be substantially quicker if we simply provided a Close button to dismiss it immediately.

But we can do even better by removing the need for input altogether. If we move this "Receipt is printing" message out of a modal and into a status icon, the interface becomes ready *by default*, allowing Morgan to move on to the next customer with no further delay or effort required.

While the "Receipt is printing" message was valuable, the blocking modal and fade-out animation stood in the way of Morgan working as smoothly as they could otherwise. By removing them, we can eliminate an unnecessary delay.

By switching this indicator to an icon in the lower left corner, Morgan is now able to move on to the next customer while the receipt is printing.

How to reduce unnecessary delays

Eliminate blocking transitions.

[See the previous example story]

Hunt down stutters and pauses.

While this modal caused a larger delay, even small interruptions can add up and be very disruptive. A delay of 10 seconds can break someone's concentration, but even delays of just over 0.3 seconds can break someone's flow.[1] Delays this small can be especially hard to find, so track these down aggressively—use speed running as a great way to uncover them (see Technique 2 in Chapter 4).

Let users leave the guided tour.

Much like the modal overlay which held Morgan hostage while it was displayed, a similar type of friction exists in guided tours. While these kinds of welcome experiences are most often meant for new users, there's usually no guarantee that a person has, in fact, never seen it before (or that they're personally getting any value from it). If you include a welcome experience, *always* seek ways to allow users to skip it.

Avoid controls that restrict a user's speed.

Lastly, watch out for controls that restrict how quickly a user can move through an interface. This happens most often in places like horizontal carousels, where holding down arrows on either side allows for scrolling through at a fixed, consistent rate, with no way to accelerate. Instead, allow users to quickly flick through the content with a scrollbar or other variable-rate input, like a swipe-to-scroll gesture.

---

1. Card, et al.

Improve speed and comfort during unavoidable delays

At the end of every month, as Morgan closed shop, they needed to generate a set of weekly reports. Because these reports were calculated from sales across the entire month, they could not be precomputed, and each took around 20 minutes to process. Even worse, the interface would only generate reports after being requested *one at a time*. This meant that each month, for a complete set of weekly reports, Morgan would need to generate each report manually—one after the other—just as soon as the previous report had finished being generated.

This got in the way as they closed shop. Morgan couldn't leave until the reports had all been generated, and each one took time to process. To shut off the device and go home, Morgan would have to stick around considerably longer than usual while they waited for things to finish.

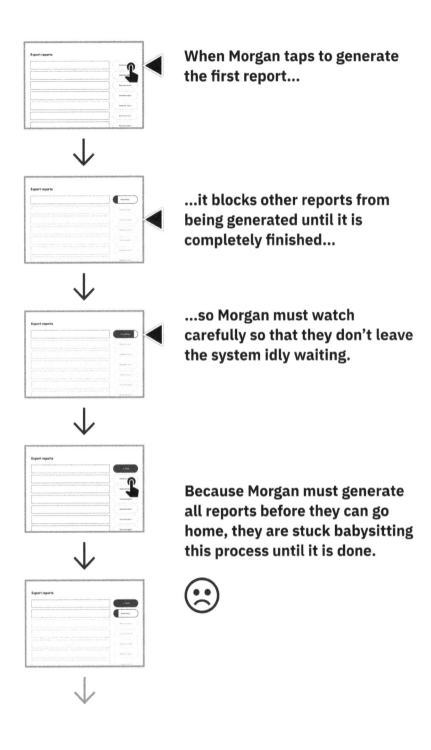

When Morgan taps to generate the first report...

...it blocks other reports from being generated until it is completely finished...

...so Morgan must watch carefully so that they don't leave the system idly waiting.

Because Morgan must generate all reports before they can go home, they are stuck babysitting this process until it is done.

Not every delay can be removed. Unfortunately, these reports could not be generated any sooner than the end of the last day of the month. But this doesn't mean that Morgan would need to stick around and babysit the process.

Instead, we can give them the ability to generate a *batch* of reports. This enables them to choose a set of reports that can be processed back-to-back automatically. Even better, we can provide the ability to have the device shut itself down automatically when everything has finished, or at a specified time, to allow Morgan to leave much earlier.

But the best part is that we can give them the ability to schedule this all to happen automatically, in advance. This means, after setting things up, Morgan would never need to deal with it again. They would be able to go home with no additional effort *in perpetuity*.

Instead, we can let them process these reports as a batch. Morgan can tap the *Add all to queue* button...

...and all reports will be generated automatically, one after the other.

Morgan can now go home without needing to babysit the process.

How to improve speed and comfort during unavoidable delays

Leverage batching, queueing, watchers, and schedulers

[See the previous example story]

Let users work in parallel during blocking tasks.

At times, it's possible to let a user start working on their next task even as the previous task is still in progress. Let's imagine Morgan needed to inspect these reports once they're generated. If they were all processed simultaneously, Morgan would need to wait for them *all* to finish before they could inspect a single one. But if the reports had instead been generated one after the other, *in sequence*, Morgan could start reviewing whichever reports had finished while the rest continued processing. Whenever there's a possibility of a user wanting to work with the results, process things in sequence (instead of all at once). In addition, consider letting users specify which item they'd like to be completed first.

Let users entertain themselves.

If a delay is *truly* disruptive, and there's absolutely no way to let a user keep going, look for ways you can help them pass the time during that delay. For any delay that you believe will last well over 10 seconds, consider providing a simple game or a light activity to make your users more comfortable as they wait.

Work with human movement

Throughout the day, Morgan would need to refill cash in the register from time to time. Doing so, however, was a bit cumbersome. To open the till, Morgan needed to press and hold a button on the screen as a security measure while turning a key with their other hand.

Unfortunately, they couldn't leave the till open and unattended, nor could they safely leave a stack of cash on the counter while doing this, so they needed to perform this two-handed maneuver while holding a large handful of cash.

This process was inherently tricky. Because of how this interface was designed, Morgan was ultimately slowed down and obstructed by the limitations of their own body.

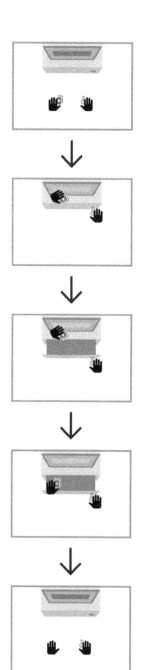

To deposit cash, Morgan must hold a large bundle of bills in their left hand & the register key in their right hand.

As a security measure, the UI requires them to hold an onscreen button while they turn the key...

...but because their left hand is already occupied with holding the cash, this is difficult to do without dropping things.

To help solve this, we have a few options. Our best bet is to reduce the number of inputs required at any one time—to allow for single-handed operation so that Morgan can perform this maneuver while holding cash safely and comfortably in their other hand.

We can do this by separating the button-holding security measure and the turning of the key into two steps. Instead of requiring both to be done simultaneously, we can allow users to press the button to create a short window of time during which the key can be turned.

Alternatively, we can allow the button-holding step to happen via a footswitch. This will allow Morgan to hold down a button with their foot and turn the key with one hand while they hold cash in the other. This helps to distribute the work more comfortably by ensuring that each part of the body is occupied with only one job at a time.

Instead, the interface can be redesigned so that each hand only does one thing at a time.

Morgan can insert the key into the register...

...then use that free hand to tap a button for a three-second countdown to unlock the register.

This way, Morgan is able to safely open the register without needing to do more than one thing with either hand at any given moment.

How to work with human movement

Accommodate for physical limitations.

[See the previous example story]

Speed things up with multiple simultaneous inputs.

While it's valuable and often critical to ensure that an interface can be used entirely with one input, like a single hand or finger, it's also possible to allow users to increase speed by using multiple inputs simultaneously. Think about the options we explored in the previous example—a timer-based unlock would allow Morgan to open the drawer entirely with one hand, but a footswitch enables them to do it *faster* by using their foot and their hand at the same time. Often, it's helpful to think of additional inputs as being a way to change the behavior of a primary input. Look for opportunities to let users make multiple inputs at once with their fingers, feet, or voice to speed things up.

Help users avoid switching input methods.

Switching between input methods—such as moving between finger and pen input or between a mouse and a keyboard—takes time and effort. Instead, for situations where someone would need to use a particular input method, provide ways to get into and out of those situations using that same input method.

Let users keep their eyes on their work.

You've seen how someone's hand can become occupied with performing a task, such as turning a key or holding onto something. Eyes are no different—we can only look at one thing at a time, and it takes a moment of effort to refocus our eyes from one area to another. Instead of depending entirely on onscreen buttons, look for ways to leverage physical controls and voice commands to let your users keep their eyes focused on their work.

Make direct paths

Whenever someone ordered an item, Morgan needed to tap to bring up the details screen and then tap the "Add to order" button. Those steps were unavoidable—even when customers wanted items as they were, with no adjustments, Morgan would still need to bring up the details screen and tap the button to continue.

Because this multistep process happened hundreds of times each day, it was needlessly fatiguing.

To add an item to the order, Morgan would need to tap the item to go to the details screen...

...then tap the *Add to order* button to add it.

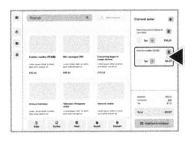

For every item ordered, Morgan would need to go through this multistep process. This was true even when a customer wanted the item without adjustments.

We can improve this substantially. Given that customers would often order items without adjustments, we can provide the ability to add menu items straight to the order by long-pressing them for a second or more.

This improves this workflow considerably by providing a direct path to a common outcome. As a result, Morgan will be able to complete orders more quickly and give customers more of their attention as they do so.

Instead, we can add the ability to tap-and-hold on an item...

...to add it to the order immediately.

Now it's much easier to add items without adjustments. This saves Morgan considerable effort over time.

How to make direct paths

Make it possible to take shortcuts.

[See the previous example story]

Ensure that the important stuff is visible.

Imagine if pricing info wasn't visible on the menu, but on the item details screen, instead. Whenever a customer asked about the price, Morgan would first need to go to this screen. This small change would be a nightmare, as it would make it harder to answer a question that gets asked hundreds of times each day. Having it visible without needing to interact makes it easier to get to, but naturally, it's overkill to show everything on the screen at once. Instead, identify the information and controls needed for the most common tasks and put them "on the surface" whenever possible. Put less commonly needed things in menus if you need the space (or consider removing them entirely).

Connect the dots to what users really want.

If a user wants to travel from page 1 to page 6, don't force them to travel through each page one at a time. Instead, give them the ability to jump to any page they like. This applies to catalog and results pages, of course, but it can also take the form of deep links into apps or websites, or shortcuts like a "Show file in source folder" option. Look for ways to let users avoid taking the long road navigationally.

Let users recycle their effort.

Sometimes, users will adjust an item in a particular way before taking steps to modify other items in the exact same way. For example, in a drawing tool, someone may want to apply the same outline and corner radius styles from one object to several others. In these cases, letting users *save or copy* the modifications from an item and *apply* them to others can spare them a lot of effort. Users get a similar benefit when they can duplicate items or swap attributes between them. Use techniques like these to let users "take a shortcut" to a result by allowing them to recycle their work or synchronize their changes across several items.

KEY POINTS TO REMEMBER

As we've just discussed, staying out of the way of our users means they can move more quickly and comfortably. This involves knowing how to manage various types of delays (either by working with them or around them), providing shorter navigational paths, and taking into account the capabilities and constraints of the human body.

UP NEXT

Ahead, we'll look at the benefits of enabling a user to predict exactly what an interface will do next and ways to design your interface to make this possible. ⊙→

8

P FOR PREDICTABLE:
HOW TO DESIGN
INTERFACES THAT LET
USERS PLAN AHEAD

A trained musician can come to know their instrument exceptionally well. With practice, they can play with their eyes closed. Their instrument is *knowable* to a great extent, and this allows for more fluid performances.

But if we were to think of modern interfaces as instruments, most of them would be extremely difficult to play. Controls often jump out of the way, or appear in inconsistent locations, or do different things depending on factors that a user can't see or control. Imagine if a pianist had to deal with all that!

Unpredictable interfaces can be *infuriating*. Trying to use an interface as elements load in bit by bit can be like trying to hit a moving target. Anyone wanting to make progress is stuck wrestling with the chaos.

By contrast, the less an interface needs to be checked or verified, the more predictable it is. Ahead, we'll look at ways that we as designers can provide consistency and allow users to anticipate exactly what will happen next.

C.U.P.I.D.

Predictable: how might we make it possible to anticipate things?

1. Create stable targets
2. Make inputs more consistent
3. Produce dependable outcomes

Create stable targets

Whenever Morgan had finished entering a customer's order, they needed to accept payment. To do this, they would need to tap the "Continue to checkout" button. This was available in the sidebar, which listed the items the customer had chosen, followed by this button.

Unfortunately, this button sat inline with the other order details. This meant the button would sit higher or lower depending on what was in the customer's order. As a result, Morgan would need to find and hit this button in its new location each time. Its location was difficult to predict in advance, so some of their attention would need to be taken away from the customer to jump through this "hoop."

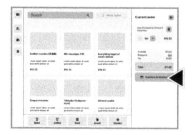

When there is one item being purchased, the *Continue to checkout* button sits about halfway down the screen...

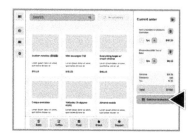

...but when there are more items being purchased, the button sits somewhere further down.

This meant that every time Morgan needed to complete a transaction, it required some of their attention to locate this button first.

The need to locate this button created a distraction every time a customer was ready to pay. By contrast, if Morgan knew where this button would be, they could move their hand into position while maintaining eye contact with their customer.

Let's give them this ability by putting this button in a fixed location. We've got three good options here. One option is to put the button *above* the order details, ensuring it will never get pushed down, no matter how long the details run. Another is to put it in a fixed "sticky" footer that always stays glued in place. Lastly, we could control the height of the order details by putting them in a scrollable area that always required the same amount of vertical space.

This way, Morgan wouldn't have to pay close attention to where the button sits and could instead give more of their attention to their customer.

Instead, we can anchor this button to the lower right corner of the screen.

No matter how many items are being purchased, the button will always be fixed in the exact same place.

Now that this button was in a more predictable spot, Morgan was no longer burdened with needing to locate this button hundreds of times each day.

How to create stable targets

Use consistent locations for actions.

[See the previous example story]

Eliminate sudden layout shifts.

As we discussed in the intro, unpredictable changes in the layout of a page as it loads content can be intensely frustrating. Often, issues like these can be solved by simply specifying the size of page elements upfront. This way, as they appear, they'll fill in the spaces set aside for them instead of shoving other content out of the way to make room. As a technical consideration, reserve space for interface elements in advance, wherever possible, and use automated tools for measuring Cumulative Layout Shift (CLS).

Ensure that you don't intercept your users' inputs.

While it can be frustrating to have content you want jump *out of the way*, it can be just as frustrating to have something unexpected jump *in front of you*. For instance, modals that appear suddenly can absorb inputs meant for other parts of the interface. Similarly, controls that show different options when being hovered over place a burden on a user's memory, as their exact location can be hard to anticipate (and properly avoid) before they appear. Never block a user with a modal unless there's an immediate action they must take before they can continue, and eliminate invisible hover-activated controls in favor of things like long-press or right-click menus, dropdowns, and shortcuts.

Make inputs more consistent

When taking a customer's order, Morgan needed to enter the customer's name using the onscreen keyboard. After typing in their name and advancing to the next screen, though, the interface would automatically "correct" what they'd entered to whatever it believed the name was supposed to be.

While this could sometimes help when Morgan had made an accidental "tap-o," it would otherwise cause problems such as changing "Kirsten" to "Kristen," changing "Nat" to "Nate," and so on. Morgan had to supervise this screen during every order to avoid these issues and keep their customers happy. All too often, they would need to undo the so-called "correction."

Every time Morgan would enter a customer's name, it would be autocorrected...

...even though the "corrections" were often wrong. This meant that Morgan frequently needed to tap to reverse these changes.

Morgan always needed to watch for mistakes made by the system. And because this extra step was not affected by skill, there was nothing Morgan could do to avoid this friction.

What's most frustrating is that practice didn't matter. At any point, there was always the possibility that *the interface* could introduce a mistake.

Thankfully, there's a simple fix. Instead of having the interface make *changes* whenever it thinks there is an issue, we can instead have it make *suggestions*, which Morgan can simply accept or ignore. This way, careful work would never be undone automatically.

In other words, we can improve this by reversing the autocorrect behavior. Rather than making users interact to "undo suggestions if they are wrong," we can instead have them interact to "accept suggestions if they are right."

This puts Morgan in control. They won't be stuck checking to see whether their input has been "auto-incorrected" again and again. Instead, their input will be accepted consistently, every time, and they'll be able to leverage suggestions at will rather than having changes pushed upon them. This way, Morgan becomes the all-powerful ruler whose word is law; the system will merely be their royal advisor, there to offer advice, not make decisions on its own.

Instead, we'll have the system accept what was entered verbatim.

Now, it will offer suggestions instead of making changes entirely on its own.

Now Morgan is only burdened with fixing *their own* mistakes, not the mistakes the system makes. The better they get at using this keyboard, the less effort it will take.

How to make inputs more consistent

Treat user input the same every time.

[See the previous example story]

Use more reliable commands.

Buttons that cycle through outcomes are harder to predict than buttons that consistently produce the same result. Think about the Clear button on a calculator—it leads to the same result every time. Users don't need to keep track of what's happening to get the desired result. Instead, they can blindly press the button—or spam it repeatedly if they want more peace of mind—and know exactly what they'll get. Look for opportunities to incorporate these dependable "uni-result" commands. In particular, watch out for situations where users may need to make a speedy selection (think of the sometimes frantic guess-and-check of a Mute/Unmute toggle vs. the trustable dependability of a single-function Mute Me button).

Make use of physical controls.

Compared to onscreen interfaces, physical controls don't blink in and out of existence—they can be pressed at any time and stay wherever they are put. Even better, users can operate them without needing to look at them, which frees their eyes to focus on more important things while they find the controls using touch and physical landmarks. Whenever possible, provide physical controls to allow users to perform their most common, high-velocity, and time-sensitive tasks with less overhead.

Produce dependable outcomes

As you may recall, on the last day of the month, Morgan needed to generate a set of weekly reports. These reports needed to go into the company's tax software but weren't generated in a format it would accept.

To get around this, an investment was made in another tool that would automatically take any reports in the wrong format, convert them to the correct format, and pass them along to the tax software. Even though this format wasn't ideal, the tool enabled a workflow that provided a seamless solution to this problem.

Sometime later, Morgan was shocked to discover that this system had suddenly stopped working. Overnight, an automatic upgrade from version 1.0 to version 1.1 was released. One key change was to the way it generated reports, as it now used a newer, more robust format. While this was otherwise a good thing, it meant that the conversion tool no longer worked correctly. As a result, the reports were no longer being sent to the tax software automatically.

Overnight, this "improvement" had managed to break their workflow, and they now had to scramble to address it immediately.

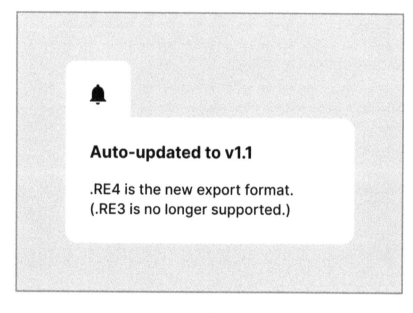

Auto-updated to v1.1

.RE4 is the new export format.
(.RE3 is no longer supported.)

The system would automatically update itself without warning, which would break certain workflows that depended on the previous outcomes.

There is little an interface can do that's more disruptive than making a user stop everything at the drop of a hat to tend to a problem that *it* caused.

Adding support for the newer format was a good thing, overall. The issue was that it switched over *irreversibly* and *without warning*.

We can do better moving forward. In situations like this, rather than changing file formats permanently and all at once, we can give users the option to choose which format they want to use (at least for some time). Giving users some flexibility in deciding when to switch lets them make changes to their workflow at a more opportune time instead of making them drop everything to address it then and there.

Sometimes, there are good reasons for making a change irreversible, but there's *almost never* a good reason to impact someone's workflow without warning. Instead, we can let users know what to expect in advance so that they can plan for it accordingly. This kind of visibility is often highly appreciated.

v2.0 is coming in 2 weeks

.RE5 will be the new default export format. If you need to, you can revert back to .RE4 or .RE3 in Settings.

Moving forward, we can give people a heads-up about disruptive changes to allow time to adjust, and provide ways to reverse these changes whenever feasible.

How to produce dependable outcomes

Offer paths to reliable results.

[See the previous example story]

Warn before removing capabilities.

We just saw how making a change to a feature can be disruptive. Similarly, it can be devastating for users who depend on one of your app's capabilities to suddenly find out it has now vanished forever. Instead, as before, let users know ahead of time if you plan to reduce the scope of what your app can do. Let them know about the proposed replacement and do what you can to help them make the switch. Approach this the way software platforms do when they deprecate an API—by warning folks ahead of time and pointing them toward alternatives. This makes it easier for users to get up to speed with the new way of doing things before the old method disappears completely.

KEY POINTS TO REMEMBER

Consistent interfaces allow users to anticipate and prepare for next steps more easily. This gives them a better sense of control, which deepens their connection to their tools and increases the likelihood they'll stick with them moving forward.

UP NEXT

Ahead, we'll look at how interfaces that require more accuracy and precision from users can be harder to use—and how we can design to be more flexible and forgiving instead. ⊙

9

I FOR INDULGENT:
HOW TO DESIGN
INTERFACES THAT ARE
MORE TOLERANT OF
MESSY INPUTS

If you asked a designer to tell you a rule about interaction design, many would tell you about Fitts's Law, which says that a target is easier to hit when it's bigger and sitting closer to you. This explains how buttons on handheld devices become easier to hit the closer they are to the thumbs of the person holding them. It even tells us why certain gestures are easier to perform than others.

If we zoom out a little, we can say that *input precision requires effort*. Interfaces become more ergonomic when they provide ways to avoid the need for precision. This applies to onscreen buttons, of course, but it's also a factor in how much time someone is given to make an input, or whether they will face consequences for getting things wrong.

When extra precision is required, extra effort is required. Ahead are some ways to allow users to get their desired results while being as free and loose with their input as possible.

C.U.P.I.D.

Indulgent: how might we accept sloppier input?

1. Leverage Fitts's Law
2. Create more tolerant inputs

Leverage Fitts's Law

Whenever Morgan would open a modal, a Close button would appear in the upper right corner of the screen. This button was the only way a modal could be dismissed. This meant that every time a modal was opened, Morgan would need to exit using this small button—it was the only way out.

It was common for Morgan to open modals several times during every transaction. Because of this, the pain of aiming for this small button added up with each order, hundreds of times each day.

To close a modal, Morgan would need to hit the Close button in the upper right.

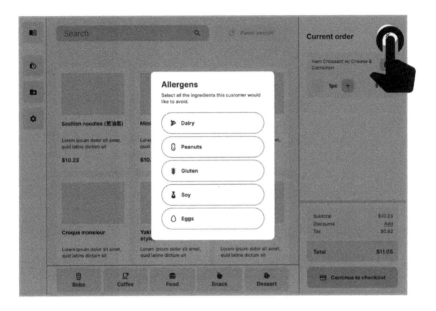

Because this button was the only way to close the modal, it formed a bottleneck. The only way to escape was to interact with that tiny tap target.

The more likely someone is to want to hit a target, the more they will benefit from it being bigger.

We can significantly reduce the effort of dismissing these modals by turning the entire area outside the modal into a tap target. Naturally, this gives Morgan a much larger area to aim for. Compared to the small Close button, this takes much less focus and precision to hit.

Now, we'll make it possible to close modals by tapping anywhere outside of them.

This is a much larger target to hit than the Close button. By removing this bottleneck, many of Morgan's workflows were improved dramatically.

How to leverage Fitts's Law

Use larger targets.

[See the previous example story]

Put things closer.

Apart from the size of the target, Fitts's Law tells us that the distance to the target is also important. This one's straightforward—try to figure out where a user's pointer is most likely to be before they use a particular control. Their pointer will often be over the control they just used, so see if you can put the next step in a process near the previous step whenever possible. This also applies to keyboard shortcuts—the shortcuts for Copy and Paste are close to each other for a reason.

Simplify inputs and gestures.

Less obviously, gestures and other complex inputs also get easier following this same logic. For example, it's easier for a user to double-tap than to tap two different points onscreen because they're already in position for the second tap. Similarly, dragging *past* a point is more lenient than dragging *to* a point. Try to replace or augment trickier inputs and gestures with broad, less demanding alternatives.

OBJECTIVE 2

Create more tolerant inputs

Whenever a customer would ask for something less common, Morgan would need to search for it.

Frustratingly, this search system only found exact matches—having even a single character out of place meant the item wouldn't appear. As a result, Morgan had to pay special attention to entering things correctly.

Additionally, it would only search for items in the current category. This meant that Morgan needed to specify the type of item before they performed their search, which required extra work.

The search interface only showed results when the search query was entered in exactly the right way.

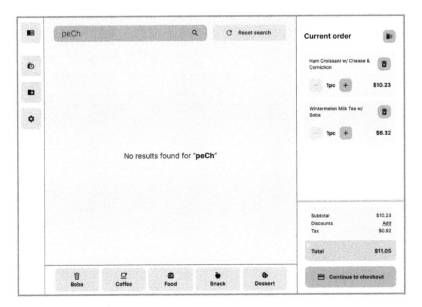

This interface required users to be precise when entering information. Morgan had to make an effort to do this correctly each time.

Because of this requirement, Morgan was forced to specify what they wanted in precise detail every time.

With our redesigned interface, we can eliminate the overhead of needing to spell words exactly right. By allowing for "fuzzy" matching, Morgan could now find "lychee" quickly, even if they'd hurriedly mistyped "luchee" instead.

Similarly, by allowing them to search across all categories by default, we can save them the effort of needing to specify a category upfront.

These changes reduce the amount of accuracy Morgan must provide, letting them spend less effort worrying about being precise and exact. As a general rule, we can make things easier by looking for ways to offer *what a user likely wants* instead of making them specify it in detail each time.

Instead, if the search doesn't find what was entered, we can try to anticipate what they might've meant.

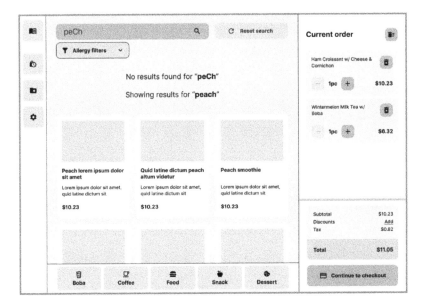

By making the interface flexible enough to handle messy input, Morgan no longer needs to spend as much of their effort being precise.

How to create more tolerant inputs

Infer what users mean.

[See the previous example story]

Watch out for time-limited interactions.

While it's harder to hit a physically smaller button than a larger one, the same principle also applies to how much time is available to take an action. When things like self-dismissing notifications and toasts are only around for a brief moment, this can increase the focus and attention needed from users who want to interact with them. When you can, remove this time pressure. For example, let users "hold" notifications by keeping them onscreen whenever a modifier key is being pressed, or provide a browsable history list to ensure they're available later.

Let users work with and around constraints.

It takes less precision to draw a shape quickly and accurately when using a stencil—it acts as a constraint, restricting a pencil to a specific area. But in reverse, systems that snap things into "correct" alignment (like *"snap-to-grid"* or similar features) can restrict a user's ability to get messy while they look for solutions they like. Find ways to let users leverage constraints in some situations and remove them in others.

Allow for mind-changing.

Users can make inputs with much less precision when the results can easily be reversed. Remember, for creative work, *the road to good runs through bad*—wrong answers are part of the game. The creative process often requires trying many things in rapid succession, which means it's much easier to find good results when the consequences of experimentation are low. Give users the ability to save, duplicate, sandbox, and undo to offer them the freedom of painless experimentation.

KEY POINTS TO REMEMBER

Interfaces that are more accommodating can reduce the burden of accuracy placed on users. By letting users make broad, general, inexact inputs, they're spared from the effort required to get things exactly right each time. Just think of the impact of something as simple as changing the size of a high-use button—it might take only a moment to make the change, but the benefit is felt in perpetuity.

UP NEXT

In our last CUPID section, we'll look at how interfaces often place burdens on a user's *mind*. By understanding what causes these burdens, we can see how to design interfaces that work *with* our minds, not *against* them. →

10

D FOR DIGESTIBLE:
HOW TO DESIGN INTERFACES THAT UNBURDEN AND RELAX THE MIND

The world is a distracting place, and focus is a limited resource. Unfortunately, a user's brainpower can come under fire from things *inside* an interface as much as anything outside. Mental burdens from a bad interface can wreak havoc on a user's overall efficiency and comfort.

Thankfully, not only can we reduce this burden, we can also create *delight*. The happier and more comfortable we can make our users, the more creatively they can think.[1] As brainpower is one of our users' most valuable resources, our goal should be to keep our users' minds relaxed and free from unnecessary stress.

C.U.P.I.D.

Digestible: how might we reduce mental strain?

1. Let users stay mentally calibrated
2. Cut down on the need to remember
3. Do the mental heavy lifting
4. Help users avoid pain
5. Tickle the mind with comfort

OBJECTIVE 1

Let users stay mentally calibrated

As a customer placed their order, Morgan would select their items and be taken to an item details screen. Adding items to an order always required navigating to this screen first. In this way, the interface was structured like rooms in a house. Morgan needed to travel from the "menu room" to the "item details room" and back again to perform this task.

---

1. Isen, A.M., Daubman, K.A., Nowicki, G.P. (1987). Positive affect facilitates creative problem solving. Journal of Personality and Social Psychology, 1122-1131.

After selecting a menu item...

...the item details would appear on a separate screen.

Entering new rooms causes people to forget things and lose their train of thought. Interfaces that require frequently moving between virtual "rooms" may make it harder to stay focused.

Interestingly, research suggests that passing through a doorway between rooms causes us to separate thoughts and events into different mental groups. Some believe this is why we often forget things when entering a new room. As this has even been shown to happen in *virtual* environments, a similar effect may also occur when moving from one screen to another.[2]

With our redesigned interface, we can eliminate the need to travel from "room" to "room" by having what Morgan needs available *where they are*. We can convert the item details screen into an item details modal. Because this can appear in context whenever it's needed, it makes it less like *going through a door* and more like *opening a drawer*.

By removing the need to travel to other virtual "rooms," we may help Morgan keep their train of thought more easily.

How to let users stay mentally calibrated

Keep things in context to avoid "virtual doorways."

[See the previous example story]

Let users keep their momentum.

Getting into the groove can take some time and effort. If a user will per-form a task with a set of items, ask yourself what will happen when they finish. Let's say they've just finished editing a batch of images—there's a good chance they'll want to continue with the next album. Look for ways to help users continue with a task once their current set of items has run out.

Keep an eye out for distractions.

Distractions are *everywhere*, and the interfaces we design are no excep-tion. The biggest culprits are delays (especially 10 seconds or more), multitasking, and things our minds are especially sensitive to (noise,

---

2. Radvansky GA, Krawietz SA, Tamplin AK. Walking through Doorways Causes Forgetting: Further Explorations. Quarterly Journal of Experimental Psychology. 2011;64(8):1632-1645. doi:10.1080/17470218.2011.571267

Instead, we can eliminate the need to travel to this other screen...

...by moving the item details into a modal.

Instead of "leaving" to get something, we can have what they need come to where they currently are. By avoiding the sensation of going to another room, we may help Morgan to stay focused.

motion, and even *faces*). Be on the lookout for distractions like these and eliminate or reduce them whenever possible.

Watch out for signal overload.

In Chapter 6 (C for Clear), we saw how stronger signals were easier to discern than more subtle ones. But this doesn't mean we should go full throttle with every signal—our attention has limits. Instead, try to strike a balance so that users don't get overwhelmed, and so the important things get the spotlight they deserve.

OBJECTIVE 2

Cut down on the need to remember

Each week, the tea stand offered a set of new specials. As these were based on the shifting prices of goods from their supplier, they would change seemingly at random from week to week.

Unfortunately, the interface didn't indicate which items were on special. Morgan needed to have the new specials memorized each week to be able to keep up.

New items were on sale every week, but the interface did not indicate which items were the current specials.

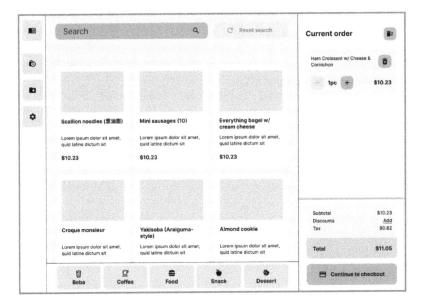

Because of this, Morgan needed to rely on their memory to be able to do their job well. This was difficult to do without making mistakes.

Because the interface didn't include this information, Morgan needed to keep it in their head. As a result, the interface was making Morgan's mind work harder than necessary.

We can fix this. In our redesigned interface, we can give Morgan the ability to tag menu items with different visual markings and see a list of these items in a centralized location. Instead of needing to remember, they can manually tag items and quickly see them at a glance.

Being able to mark items in different ways also provides other benefits. Morgan can now set shortcuts for their regular customers' orders and quickly mark items that have run out of stock. As a result, this gives Morgan a way of "jotting down a note to themselves" in the UI, which lets them save their mental energy for other things.

By providing the ability to mark menu items with a star, Morgan could spot the current specials at a glance.

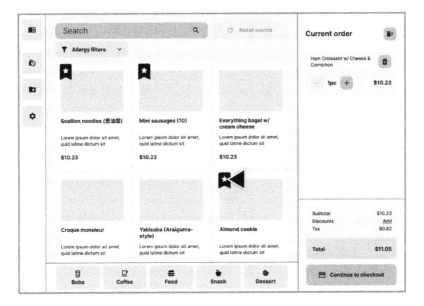

Now, the information Morgan needs is on the screen. This reduces their mental burden and allows them to give more attention to their customer.

How to cut down on the need to remember

Allow for and provide contextual clues.

[See the previous example story]

Make mappings familiar.

A "mapping" is the relationship between a control and an outcome. "Natural mappings" are a way of connecting the dots between a control and what it does by baking information about how it works *into the control itself.* These can be *spatial* (like arranging controls in the same layout as the things being controlled), *behavioral* (like silencing an alarm by covering it with a hand), or *conceptual* (like the relationship between a volume slider going up and the audio getting louder). Intuitive mappings like these allow our minds to process them more quickly.[3] Look for natural mappings and use them whenever you can.

Offer direct comparisons.

Choosing between items is difficult if you can't directly compare your options. Without this ability, you're forced to try to recall details about one option while you inspect the other. This reliance on memory increases mental effort and leads to worse results. Instead, when users need to evaluate their options, allow them to compare *directly* using side-by-side comparisons, blended/overlapping comparisons, and instant toggling (crucially, with no intermediate loading state lasting more than 50–100ms).

Watch out for behavior that defies expectations.

Imagine an app where the "Send" and "Delete" icons have been swapped—it's an extreme example, but icons in icon libraries are often applied incorrectly. When things don't work as a user has come to expect, they'll need to learn this unusual behavior. But they are *also* saddled with remembering that this particular app works differently from the others they know. Interestingly, while the effort of *learning*

---

3. Norman, Donald A. The Design of Everyday Things: Revised and Expanded Edition. Basic Books, 2013.

may go away, the effort of *remembering what's different here* sticks around. When using components or processes users may already be familiar with, avoid breaking with convention whenever possible (and provide strong warnings whenever this can't be avoided).

Do the mental heavy lifting

Occasionally, Morgan would get asked if a menu item contained certain allergens. Unfortunately, while each item did include a list of ingredients, there was no easy way to see which allergens a given item might include. To answer this question, Morgan needed to carefully go through the list of ingredients to look for any allergens that might be relevant.

When a customer wanted to avoid certain allergens, Morgan needed to look through the ingredient list.

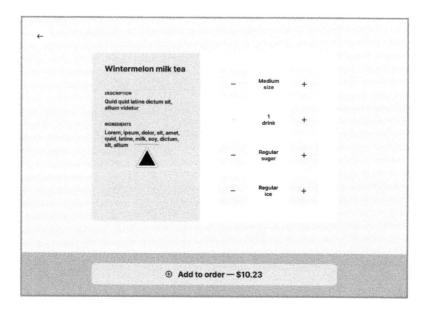

Morgan has the data, but the information they need isn't readily obvious. This puts a cognitive burden on them to complete the order correctly.

Remember, the information Morgan needs *already exists*, but it's in a format that's hard for them to access. But while it can be tricky for a person to find an item in a list, it's easy for a machine to do it, which means this process should be a breeze.

In the new interface, we can give Morgan the ability to filter down the menu whenever someone wants to avoid a particular ingredient. This way, instead of doing the mental work of reading and parsing items one by one, they can simply tap a button to see the appropriate results.

Instead, we can allow allergens to be filtered out to remove this mental burden.

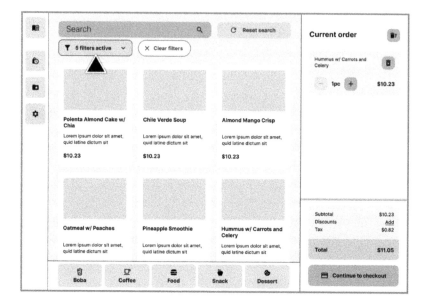

Now that Morgan has the ability to hide all items that contain certain allergens, they can give customers what they need with less effort.

How to do the mental heavy lifting

Allow for sorting and filtering.

[See the previous example story]

Summarize with context.

When a user has a lot of data to go through, they may find it valuable to have a summary with the information they need front and center. But that's often not enough—if all they had was a summary, it might leave them wishing they could look at the greater context to help them fill in the gaps in their understanding. Whenever presenting users with a lot of data, create a summary, and deliver it alongside access to the whole story. This way, they can both get an overview and do a deeper dive when they want to.

Help users avoid pain

Morgan often needed to open shop at 5:30 AM. Like most people, they weren't at their sharpest at this hour, making them more error-prone than at other times during the day. The same was true when they were burnt out at the end of a long shift. This fatigue made certain tasks inherently more risky.

At the start and end of their shift, Morgan wasn't nearly as mentally sharp. So when they would quickly ring up a customer...

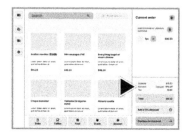

...they may not realize if they've accidentally added a discount.

Morgan was always at higher risk of making mistakes at certain points in their shift, but the interface didn't do anything to accommodate for this.

By identifying situations where Morgan is more likely to make mistakes, we can find opportunities to provide safeguards.

With a Sleepy Mode, Morgan can enable extra checkpoints for actions that might have a bad outcome if done by mistake, such as marking the wrong item as being out of stock or issuing an incorrect discount. They can even schedule these to turn on automatically at the beginning or end of their shift so they'll get this help without needing to remember first.

Somewhat counterintuitively, Morgan can reduce their *overall* effort by putting some *additional* effort between themselves and a bad outcome. While Morgan doesn't need these safeguards when they feel sharp and alert in the middle of their shift, being able to turn on safety precautions like these helps them avoid mistakes when they are most vulnerable.

Instead, by allowing Morgan to enable a Sleepy Mode at certain times of day...

...they can now require a PIN for certain actions, like adding discounts, so that they can avoid doing them accidentally.

Now that Morgan can set up guardrails at times they wanted to be especially careful, they can spend less effort recovering from mistakes when they're at highest risk.

How to help users avoid pain

Keep mental states in mind.

[See the previous example story]

Introduce friction as "guardrails" where necessary.

We've just seen how adding friction to an interaction can be helpful when users aren't feeling their sharpest. But there are many things even a clear-minded individual would want to avoid doing acciden-tally—like opening the till or shutting the device off. In cases like these, where the outcome can be especially harsh or time-consuming to fix, it's better to have users perform a simple task as a safeguard. Options include doing something that starts a process (like a button that kicks in only after it is held for a moment) or something that stops the process when it is no longer being done (like a button that only keeps a process going while it's being pressed).

Free your users from fear.

Things are trickier when there is a fear of consequences. Common fears include a fear of data loss, of social embarrassment, or of personal or professional safety. Try to identify the negative outcomes your users may be fearing in a given situation, and look for ways you can mitigate those fears. Sometimes, a reassuring message (like "Your files are backed up automatically") is all it takes.

Tickle the mind with comfort

This register was themed in a distinctive shade of purple. The designer had done a good job here—the color had no issues with legibility and was liked by most people.

But it distracted Morgan. There's no way the designer could have known it, but this particular shade of purple took Morgan back to their classroom in the 3rd grade, where they had to deal with some pretty tough bullying. It might seem silly, but it didn't change the fact that it bothered Morgan each time they used it.

Previously, the interface was only available with a consistent visual treatment for all users.

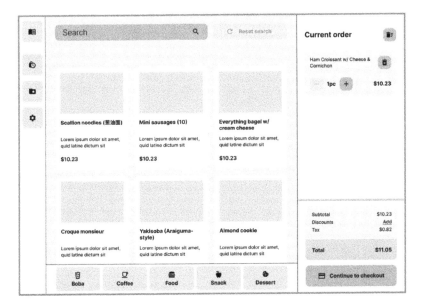

When a digital workspace doesn't allow for any customization, it prevents users from being as comfortable as they might otherwise be.

While this can seem like a minor gripe, it was a real source of discomfort for Morgan, and it affected their ability to be fully focused whenever they used the interface. Ultimately, this isn't about the color purple, but about the peace of mind users can enjoy when they can customize their environment to make themselves more comfortable.

To help accommodate this, we can provide the ability to change the color scheme. So that users don't paint themselves into a corner, we can put smart limits on how far things can be modified and take special care to ensure that no accessibility issues can be introduced with the options available. We'll also add a "reset" feature to make it easier to start over.

For the most robust solution, we can also give them easy ways to share custom themes with others. This allows better solutions to go viral, which can save users even more time and effort.

Instead, we can allow Morgan to adjust the visuals to their liking, within reasonable limits, such as by providing a Dark Mode.

By enabling some degree of control over the visual appearance, Morgan can now feel a greater sense of autonomy and mental comfort than before.

How to tickle the mind with comfort

Improve aesthetics and accommodate individual preferences.

[See the previous example story]

Provide flexibility where you can.

Workflows that follow a strict sequence using a fixed set of inputs are often less ergonomic than more flexible options. Try to let users work around parts of a process that cannot be undone, reversed, or performed out of order. Do an Interaction Cost Analysis (ICA) as described in Chapter 4 and look for opportunities to allow a user to perform a step from later in the process ahead of time. This can often be done by letting users specify their own shortcuts like gestures, key combinations, voice commands, etc. (as before, it's even better when these can be saved, synced, and shared with others).

Help users feel oddly satisfied.

Lastly, try to create what might be called an unusual sense of satisfaction. We seem to love seeing order come out of chaos—especially when things start out ordered, become chaotic, and resolve to a new order. We also relish the feeling of closure that comes when the last piece of a puzzle slides snugly into place. In particular, look for ways to give users this feeling by giving them big, visually impressive outcomes from small amounts of input and by celebrating moments of completion.

KEY POINTS TO REMEMBER

It's time to celebrate our own moment of completion—you've made it!

In this final chapter, you've seen how mental burdens can get in the way. The more we can make someone feel comfortable and relaxed, the more smoothly and confidently they can move through an interface, while making fewer mistakes along the way.

PART III
APPENDICES

A

THE USABILITY MATRIX:
HOW TO COMPARE INTERFACES BASED ON THEIR USABILITY

As we've discussed throughout this book, different types of effort make apps attractive in different ways. In overly broad terms:

- Better learnability makes things easier on the first run.
- Better ergonomics make things easier in the long run.

This knowledge gives us new tools we can use for improving ease of use. In Chapter 3, we saw how to apply this to make individual features as easy to use as possible. Now, we'll zoom out and see how this can help you decide *which* features to build and in *which order*.

In an ideal world, we'd get to build everything we'd like to, but time and resources are limited. Instead, by applying this framework, we can make strategic decisions about the improvements we make. Doing this helps us narrow in on the most impactful changes we can make with our available resources.

Over time, I started using what I call a Usability Matrix. It's a tool that helps show how different interfaces compare in terms of learning and ergonomic effort. With it, you can make smarter decisions about which changes you prioritize. This helps you to give your users the most benefit you can at any given point. It also shows you where you're most vulnerable to losing users and reveals opportunities to attract new ones.

This is valuable for helping you and your team set priorities. But it also enables you to share and explain your priorities with stakeholders using a simple visual.

Each type of effort affects users in different ways

Earlier, we discussed how each type of effort affects users differently. It's worth taking a moment here to underscore how this will impact their decisions.

Better learnability can attract new users

There's a simple reason learnability gets so much of our attention, and it's a good one: a user can't get any benefit out of an interface they can't figure out. When an app is easy to grasp, people can benefit from it sooner. In short, good learnability lowers the barrier to entry and makes things attractive to users with less experience and lighter use cases.

However, as we've discussed, the longer someone uses an app, the less learning effort will affect them each day.

Better ergonomics can attract new users, too

Though it might be less obvious, it's possible for better ergonomics to draw in new users, as well. Let's explore this for a moment.

Whenever a big tech company announces a new product, some folks quickly become unhappy with what they already use. This happens even if they were happy with what they were using up until then. As soon as they understand how the new product will make it easier for them to reach their goals, it can be hard for them to want to keep doing things the way they did before.[1]

Sometimes, a new product won't actually solve any new problems. In these cases, it's simply offering a new way to solve a problem that people are already solving in another way. But people will still get excited about this, even if they *already know* another way to get those results. In other words, it's usually not exciting to them because it's easier to learn. Instead, the main benefit comes from ergonomic effort.

As demonstrated in Chapter 3, when a user knows a better way exists, doing it the old way can feel like a waste of effort. This will often feel more painful when they know they'll use it a lot. So, as discussed in

---

1. Sidenote: People usually get excited about a new product because it makes reaching their goals easier. Sometimes, they get excited because it's shiny and new, and that makes them feel good. But even "feeling good" is a goal in and of itself, and this new gadget will make it easier for them to achieve that goal. We'll go into more detail about that in the next section, Appendix B. But we'll set it aside for now to keep things focused.

Chapter 2, this is more affected by how much a user *expects* to use it, not by how much they *currently* use it.

In other words, folks don't need to have used a product before to get excited by how much time and effort it will save them. People don't need to be experts to appreciate better ergonomics; because of this, improving it can help draw in new users.

Better ergonomics can keep users around

Once someone gets up to speed with a highly ergonomic solution, getting them to switch can be very difficult.

A great example of this is a text editor called Vim. If you haven't heard of Vim, that's OK. All you need to know is that it's a text editor that has been around for what seems like forever and is known for being *absurdly* difficult to learn. It's so famously hard to figure out that one of the top searches for it is "How do I quit the Vim editor?"—even *quitting* is confusing.

It can be overwhelming to get started with Vim. (Credit: Wikimedia Commons)

But even though Vim is hard to learn, watching someone who knows how to use it is like watching a smooth performance by an expert ballet dancer or a trained musician. I remember being amazed as my coworker Gordon used it to fly through several files and edit multiple lines of text in each of them *at once*. It was fluid, elegant, and graceful.

Because of this, it's clear why so many Vim users love it so much, often to a fanatical degree. They have earned a reputation for how passionately they defend it. Vim has a truly cult-like following, with some even describing it as "a way of life."

This app can almost certainly be made easier to learn, and there's virtually no chance this would currently make it through "first-look" usability testing. But we must remember that while learnability is valuable, *it isn't enough*. In cases where the app will be used for many hours, day after day, the ergonomic benefits matter a lot more to users. The more they expect to use it, the more incentive they have to invest time in learning it.

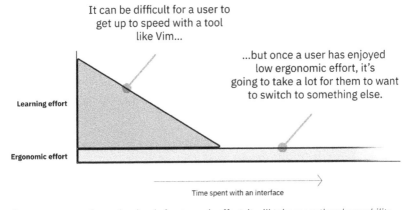

It can be difficult for a user to get up to speed with a tool like Vim...

...but once a user has enjoyed low ergonomic effort, it's going to take a lot for them to want to switch to something else.

Learning effort

Ergonomic effort

Time spent with an interface

Once someone enjoys a low level of ergonomic effort, it will take more than learnability improvements to make them want to switch to something else.

Yes, an app that's easier to learn is easier to get started with. But for these users to want to switch to another tool, the alternative can't just be easier to learn. It must require less ongoing effort than what they already use.

The ergonomics of this app have made it stickier and harder to quit.

To sum up, good learnability makes it easier to get in the door, but for regular use, good ergonomics provide the incentive to go through the door—and stay there.

A power tool for visualizing interface strengths and weaknesses

Let's put all that to practical use.

The Usability Matrix is a powerful tool that combines much of what this book has covered.

To get us started, here's an empty Usability Matrix:

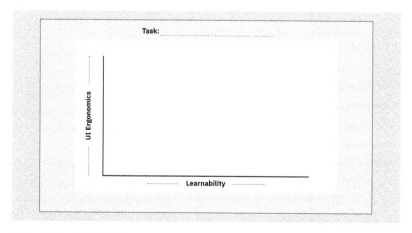

An empty Usability Matrix.

Comparing proposed interface changes

Let's look at how to use a Usability Matrix to compare various proposed app improvements. As mentioned earlier, this can be valuable for helping you see which direction will be a better use of your time and resources.

Imagine we are working on an early-stage app for page layout and design that is still relatively "bare-bones." To use it, users must click tools in a toolbar for doing things like drawing shapes and text boxes and to access tools for repositioning them.

Given the needs of our imaginary users, the primary task we are concerned with is *designing a small poster.* This involves selecting several different tools from the toolbar to complete the task.

In our example, we can imagine that there are proposals for two distinct design directions to take the product in:

- "The Wizard"—A system that walks users through creating a suitable poster one step at a time.
- "Shortcuts"—A system for allowing users to simplify the process of switching tools through keyboard commands.

Imagine that this is a small team building this app, and resources are constrained, so we won't have the luxury of building both options at once. We'll need to decide what to build first, so illustrating this with a Usability Matrix can help make the differences and strengths of each option more readily apparent.

Let's start by preparing our Usability Matrix:

1. **Grab some sticky notes (real or virtual).** This will make it easier to reposition things as you go through the process.

2. **Draw a Usability Matrix.** Do this by drawing a 2 × 2 matrix (a large right-angle), and then write "Learnability" on the X axis and "UI Ergonomics" on the Y axis.

3. **Write the task you're using to compare as the title.** Here, we'll write "Designing a small poster" as the title.

4. **Write "Current version" on a sticky note and place it in the center of the matrix.** It can be helpful to use a different color or shape to make the current version of the app easier to distinguish from other options.

5. **Put each of the other design directions on individual sticky notes.** Here, we'll write "The Wizard" and "Shortcuts" on separate notes.

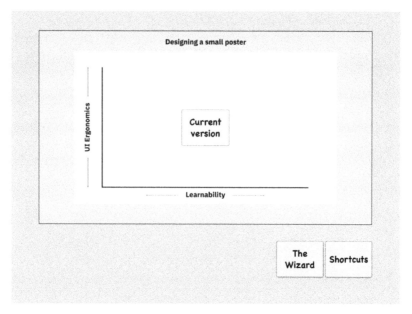

To help you illustrate the advantages of interface changes relative to what you already have, start by creating sticky notes for each approach and place the sticky note representing the interface you currently have in the center of the matrix.

Picking up each sticky note individually, we'll compare it to the other options currently in the matrix. Let's start by evaluating learnability. To do this, we'll ask:

> *"Comparing the approaches on these sticky notes, which one provides users with a more intuitive way of completing this task?"*

In other words, which option provides the better Most Learnable Path (MLP)? Here's how we can answer in this case:

- "The Wizard"—Because this offers a more intuitive way of designing a poster, this would provide an option that is more inherently learnable than the other options available. (Better Learnability.)
- "Shortcuts"—Because these shortcuts would not be as inherently obvious as the toolbar or the wizard, this would not provide an option that improves the overall learnability of completing this task. But because the toolbar would still be available, the MLP would be the same as what's available in the current version. (Same Learnability.)

Next, we'll evaluate UI Ergonomics in a similar way. To do this, we'll ask:

"Comparing what's on both of these sticky notes, which one provides users with a more ergonomic way of completing this task?"

In other words, which option provides the better Most Ergonomic Path (MEP)? It's usually easy to estimate this, but if you need help, Chapter 4 offers advice for doing this. Here's how we answer:

- "The Wizard"—This walks users through the process of creating a poster step-by-step, which requires more ergonomic effort than the toolbar. But because the toolbar will still be available, the MEP will be the same as in the current version, so the minimum ergonomic effort required won't change. (Same UI Ergonomics.)
- "Shortcuts"—This gives users a way to switch between tools without taking their mouse away from their work to click icons in the toolbar. As a result, it offers a more ergonomic option than using the toolbar or the wizard. (Better UI Ergonomics.)

We'll place the approaches that offer better learnability further to the right and put the approaches that offer better UI Ergonomics further up. That should look like this:

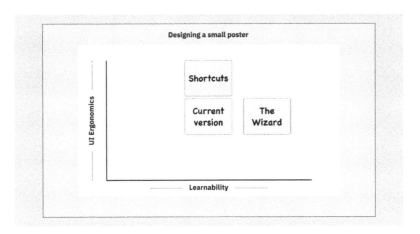

A completed Usability Matrix showing the differences in effort required for completing a task ("Designing a small poster") using three different approaches. Approaches sitting further up are more ergonomic, while those sitting further right are more learnable.

What the positions mean

With these examples, we start to understand how different positions tell us different things. Let's quickly recap some of what we covered earlier about how each type of effort affects users and the decisions they make:

	BETTER LEARNABILITY (X axis / Things further to the right)	BETTER ERGONOMICS (Y axis / Things sitting further up)
WHO VALUES THIS THE MOST?	Less experienced users tend to value this the most, as it helps them get in the door and up to speed.	More experienced users value this the most, as they are no longer dealing with as much learning effort.
WHO VALUES THIS THE LEAST?	More experienced users largely don't care about this once they've already learned.	While still valuable to less experienced users, this is often less appreciated by them unless they are familiar with a different approach (such as when they switch from a competing product).
FREQUENCY OF USE	This is more valuable to users who expect lighter or infrequent use cases (e.g., non-daily users).	This is valued by those who expect heavy use cases (e.g., daily users). These users have a strong pull toward more ergonomic options; they are highly resistant to moving to a less ergonomic option.
WHERE IT'S MOST VALUABLE IN-APP	This is a better starting point for less commonly used interactions (like a settings screen).	This is most valuable for interactions that accumulate a lot of usage (like a toolbar).

As a good rule of thumb, users want options sitting as far to the right as possible (though less experienced users care about this more). Users also want options placed further up, and the more they think they'll use it, the more willing they are to move further to the left to access higher options. The top right corner is ideal, and the bottom left corner is what I like to call the "Zone of Pain."

In broad terms, people want things sitting *toward the right*, and the more they expect to use something, the more the center of gravity shifts *toward the top*.

With this in mind, we can see that because *The Wizard* is sitting to the right:

- It would be most valuable to newer users and those with lighter use cases.
- It would be shrugged off by many experienced users and those with heavier use cases.

Because *Shortcuts* is sitting higher up:

- It would be valued most by more experienced users and those with heavier use cases.
- It would be shrugged off by many newer users and those with lighter use cases.
- It would provide a lot of benefit due to how common the task of switching tools is.

This can help you have more informed discussions about the tradeoffs of each of your options. The right thing to build will ultimately come down to the priorities of your team and your users, and this can help everyone get on the same page to have that discussion.

As with many design exercises, you can do this independently, although you may find it more beneficial to do it with your team or invite stake-holders to participate. If you decide to do it as a group, make sure that everyone involved understands how to quickly estimate ergonomic effort—see the section on performing an Interaction Cost Analysis (ICA) in Chapter 4 if you need help.

Comparing competing products

Next, let's look at how we can use this to compare our app against various competing products. To do this, we follow the same general process as before. We will choose a task, create sticky notes for each product, and ask which option can be used to complete the task with the least amount of learning or ergonomic effort.

For this example, let's imagine that the app we are designing is no longer "bare-bones" and is relatively competitive in the market. We'll follow a similar process to the one we just followed, with some slight adjustments.

Let's start by preparing our Usability Matrix:

1. **Grab some sticky notes (real or virtual).**

2. **Draw a Usability Matrix, and title it with the task you're using as the basis of comparison.** Here, we'll write "Designing a small poster" as the title once again.

3. **Write "Our product" on a sticky note.** Don't place it in the matrix just yet. As before, using a note of a different color or shape can help make your product easier to distinguish.

4. **Put each of your main competitors for this task on their own sticky notes.** Here, we'll write "App A," "App B," and "App C" on separate sticky notes.

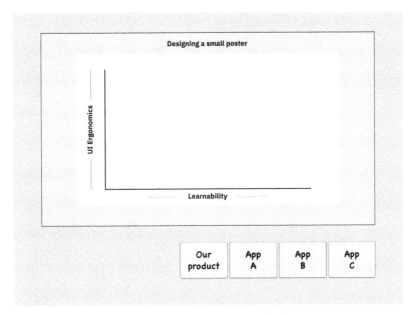

When comparing a larger number of options, going through the process more methodically can be beneficial. Start by creating sticky notes for each option you're comparing, but don't place anything in the matrix just yet.

Next, we'll determine how each option compares to each other, as we did in the last example. When comparing many options, using a slightly more systematic process may be valuable. We'll walk through that process now.

Start by picking up a pair of sticky notes and determining how they compare to each other. As before, we'll evaluate learnability first. To do this, we'll ask the same question as before:

> *"Comparing what's on both of these sticky notes, which one provides users with a more* intuitive *way of completing this task?"*

In this example, we'll say that we believe our product is easier to learn than App A when it comes to completing this task. Next, attach the sticky notes in their relative horizontal positions in the space just below the matrix, with more learnable options sitting further to the right. It should look something like this:

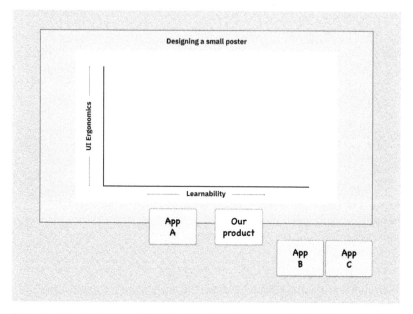

Determine the relative learnability of each option. Compare a pair of options and ask which approach is easiest to figure out when completing the specified task, and then place the winning option further right.

As we pick up the remaining sticky notes, we'll ask this same question regarding each sticky note we've already attached beneath the Usability Matrix one at a time. This will allow you to determine the relative learnability of each option systematically.

Remember that two options can be tied. When this happens, attach one sticky note to the end of another. In this example, we can imagine that App B and App C are both using a nearly identical approach that is highly learnable, which puts them in a tie for first place. We'll attach their sticky notes together so that they share the same horizontal position:

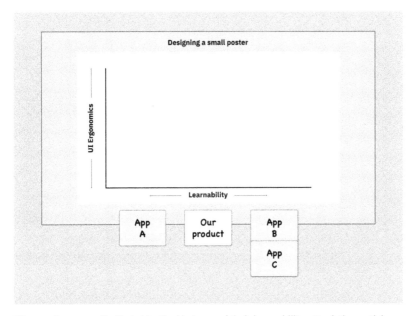

If two options are effectively identical in terms of their learnability, attach those sticky notes end-to-end so that they share the same horizontal position.

Next, we'll evaluate UI Ergonomics in a similar way. To do this, start with a pair of sticky notes and ask:

> *"Comparing what's on both of these sticky notes, which one provides users with a more ergonomic way of completing this task?"*

(As before, it's usually easy to estimate this, but if you need help, Chapter 4 offers techniques for doing this.)

Since you've already determined how far left or right each option will sit in the matrix, all that remains is to determine how high or low each option will sit. Move each sticky note directly up into position as you go through this process. You should be left with something that looks a bit like this:

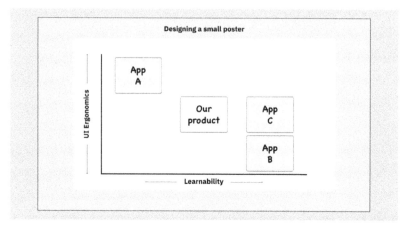

After determining their horizontal positions, repeat the process to find their vertical positions. Do this by asking how inherently ergonomic each option is for this task relative to the others, and then place the winners further up.

As before, we can infer conclusions about each item in the matrix based on their relative positions. It can be helpful to reference the section "What the positions mean" earlier in this appendix to make this easier.

Here are some conclusions we might draw from this regarding the task we've chosen:

- App A sits above and to the left of our product. Because we sit further right, our product is more attractive to users with less experience and lighter use cases. And because their product sits further up, it's more appealing to more experienced users and users with heavier use cases. If our users consider this task important, they may leave for App A as they gain more experience. Our best bet is to improve the UI Ergonomics of completing this task in our product to a similar or better level.
- Our product sits above and to the left of App B, so we're in a similar situation as with App A, but in reverse. This time, *their* product is

more attractive to users with less experience and lighter use cases. In contrast, *our* product is more appealing to more experienced users and users with heavier use cases.

- App C, though, poses a threat to us. They sit directly to our right, meaning users with less experience will find their product more attractive than ours. And while we might hope to attract users from App B as they gain experience, App C offers similar ergonomic benefits while *also* being easier to learn. This is a one-two punch. More experienced users fleeing App B for better UI Ergonomics will consider App C a worthy alternative to our app. Combine this with the fact that less experienced users are also more likely to choose App C, and it means we're vulnerable on two fronts.

- App A is a problem, too. Remember that more experienced users are averse to switching to something with worse UI Ergonomics (see Chapter 3), so we're unlikely to attract many users from App A either. Our best bet is to either offer a more ergonomic method so that we at least match App A or to improve our learnability so that we at least match App B and App C. If we have the time and budget, doing both would place us in the upper right, making our option the most attractive for this task.

While this has helped us determine how our app compares to our competitors through the lens of this task, remember that many products, if not most, don't live and die by the ability to complete a *single* task. To get a clearer picture of where you stand in terms of effort, create a separate Usability Matrix for each of the key tasks you believe are most important to your users.

Choosing tasks with care is vital

The secret to getting good results with a Usability Matrix is to use care when choosing which task you are basing the comparison on. This is important because the task determines which options can be compared and where they sit relative to each other.

For example, while we chose to compare the task of *designing a small poster*, simply changing this to *designing a small poster with Pantone-managed colors* may have changed things completely. Some options may have become much harder to figure out, others may have a massive change to the ergonomic effort involved, and others may not support this at all and would be left out of the conversation.

So, it's essential to use care when choosing which task to use in your comparison. These tasks should be as closely aligned with your users' goals as possible, and simply speaking with those users should help you narrow in on a good set. Tasks should also be as precisely defined as possible, so while we're using short examples here, it's usually better to use a lengthier description.

KEY POINTS TO REMEMBER

The Usability Matrix is a tool you can use to compare different interfaces in terms of the effort they require. It helps you visualize usability strengths and weaknesses and allows for making more intelligent decisions about what to build for users.

Ultimately, this allows you to make the most of your team's resources by making changes in a targeted way.

TRY THIS

- **Pick tasks wisely.** Talk with your users, and identify the tasks that are most important to them. These will serve as the basis for your comparisons, so take your time to get these right.

- **Use a Usability Matrix to visualize the pros and cons of different options.** This is especially helpful when there is disagreement over which changes will be most impactful.

continues

- **To find strategic opportunities, use a Usability Matrix to evaluate where you sit with regard to competitors.** Do this by evaluating the tasks your users care the most about. Use it to spot opportunities to move your app into a better strategic position by making targeted improvements to either type of effort.

- **Use a hybrid approach to evaluate how proposed product features will affect where you sit relative to your competitors.** This can help you better understand how these proposed changes will impact your positioning so that you can invest your efforts where they will be most effective.

- **Learn to do this in your head.** Practice estimating where different products might sit in relationship to each other. Earlier, we discussed how the text editor Vim is famously hard to learn while offering outstanding UI Ergonomics. Compared to a generic text editor, where could each option sit in a Usability Matrix for the task of *coding a website*? Also, going back to Chapter 3, how might we position A) an interface that only offers the text-driven search interface, versus B) one that only offers the graphical search interface, versus C) an interface that offers both options for the task of *completing a search*? See if you can do this in your head, and use the process described in this chapter if you need to double-check your answer. See this footnote for the answers.[2]

---

2. "Coding a website": For this task, the generic text editor would likely be much easier to figure out, but Vim would be much more ergonomic. This would mean the generic text editor could be placed in the lower right, while Vim could be placed in the upper left. "Completing a search": For this task, Option A would offer the better MEP, while Option B would offer the better MLP, and Option C would offer both the better MLP and MEP. Here, we can put Option A against the top edge, Option B against the right edge, and Option C in the top right corner.

B

THE PRODUCT PYRAMID:

A MODEL FOR UNDERSTANDING USER BEHAVIOR AND PRIORITIES

Throughout this book, we've looked at elements that influence what makes a person pick one app over another. When I discuss this topic with others, it's common for the conversation to turn to other factors that affect user choice and how each factor relates to the others.

In these discussions, I keep returning to a particular mental image. For the sake of conversation, we'll call this the Product Pyramid. It has been useful for helping to anticipate what a user is likely to do when you know their priorities. But it's also extremely valuable to use it *in reverse*—by looking at user behavior and working backward to reveal what their true priorities are.

In broad terms, the aim of a product is to make it easier for a certain audience to achieve their goals. As such, when that audience doesn't show much interest, it's an indication that there are issues of some sort. The Product Pyramid is a tool that makes it easier to identify exactly where the problem is, so you can make targeted improvements to correct the issue without going back to the drawing board and starting from scratch.

Since this is a model, I'm reminded of the expression, "All models are wrong, but some models are useful." I'm likely wrong about some element, and this model is no doubt imperfect in some way. Nevertheless, I have found this model useful for the reasons mentioned. I hope it also proves useful to you (or, at the very least, helps to spark a healthy debate).

Here's a preview of the diagram we'll be exploring:

The Product Pyramid

The Principle of Least Effort

The Product Pyramid centers around the Principle of Least Effort (also known as Zipf's Law). To summarize, this principle states the following:

> *People try to reduce the total amount of effort needed to reach all their goals, to the best of their knowledge, now and into the future.*

There is some debate about whether this *determines* the actions people take or if it merely reveals which actions we *are inclined* to take. But it doesn't really matter to us; for our purposes, this is a distinction without much of a difference. In either case, it gives us a highly reliable way to anticipate what users are likely to do.

In short, this seems to indicate that users choose tools based on the following:

- *Complete Goal Set* (all of their goals)
- *User Understanding* (what they know about their options)
- *Capabilities* (whether a given option can provide the results they need)
- *Effort* (what it will take to get those results)

Let's build a pyramid

The diagram we'll create is similar in structure to Maslow's Hierarchy of Needs. In case you're not familiar, it's a pyramid-shaped diagram that puts food, shelter, and other basic human needs at the bottom and loftier goals and aspirations at the top. We'll do something similar by stacking each layer in our diagram in order of relative importance. Let's look at each level.

Complete Goal Set

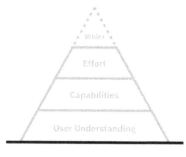

Complete Goal Set

It's important to remember that while your product will help users reach *some* of their goals, their true aim is to reduce their overall effort in reaching *all* their goals. So, while a noisy leaf blower can help someone achieve their goal of keeping their yard clean, it might run afoul of their other goal of keeping their neighbors happy. In other words, we must remember that user goals always have a broader context.

I put a user's goals as the ground beneath the pyramid; it's the bigger context the pyramid fits into.

User Understanding

According to the Principle of Least Effort, users make decisions based on *what they know about their options*. This means that when examining why a user would choose one product over another, we must contend with what a person *understands* about a product before we can even evaluate the product itself.

A user will decide based on the best of their knowledge, which means that if they aren't aware of the advantages of one product versus another, it can't play into their decision. It also means that users can be mistaken, which can lead to them choosing products that are less well-suited to their needs.

Bear this in mind when trying to understand why users would choose a tool you believe is not the best suited for their use case. While it's entirely possible that you haven't fully understood their needs, it's also quite possible that they are misinformed about the options available to them.

LEVEL TWO

Capabilities

Next, we have what I call *capabilities*. These are all the things a given product can be used for.

Think back to the Usability Matrix in Appendix A. In it, we compared several tools based on a task they could each complete. Importantly, to make this comparison, the tool doesn't need to be intended to be used for that task. All that matters is that it is *capable* of being used for that task. In other words, a tool's capabilities are defined by the tasks it can complete.

Users will only consider using a tool if they believe it can provide the results they need. Capabilities are therefore tied to needs, which means they can depend on things like speed (e.g., "I need to do this 300 times per hour") and quality (e.g., "I need to be able to capture clear images of the Aurora Borealis"). Note that they can be *quantitative* or *qualitative*, as some needs depend on subjective assessment.

This also means that when you decide what your product will be capable of, you are effectively defining who your competition is. This ultimately determines who you'll be compared against, so be mindful of what your product can be used for. While adding new capabilities can open your product to more users and use cases, it can also diminish how a product is perceived if any of these use cases aren't handled well.

LEVEL THREE

Effort

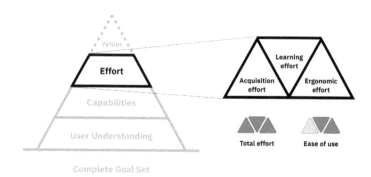

On the third level of our pyramid, we account for all the effort of getting and using an interface.

This comes in three types. Throughout this book, we've looked at the effort of using a product, which we've been breaking apart into *learning effort* and *ergonomic effort*. These are a measure of usability, or ease of use. But we also need to account for the friction involved with acquiring the product *before* it can be used. For lack of a better term, we'll call this *acquisition effort*.

Acquisition effort

These are all the efforts of "getting" a product. Most obviously, this would include the cost. It also includes any effort to transport, set up, or configure the product so that it can be used. For a free app, this effort is often negligible. But it can be substantial in some situations, so remember to account for it.

Learning effort

To summarize what we've discussed earlier, *learning effort* is most pronounced at the start of a given user's experience with a product. It then tends to diminish over time.

The primary exceptions to this are when users need to relearn parts of an interface that have been forgotten (which is most common with interfaces that are used sporadically, with significant gaps of time in between) and when an interface is redesigned in a way that changes how it is used (which can introduce new learning effort months or even years later).

Because learning doesn't happen in a vacuum, users can transfer some of what they know about one product to another. This means that different users will face different amounts of remaining effort at the start of their experience with a new interface.

So, as you account for this effort, remember how it varies per user and over time. Because of this, when evaluating an interface using a Usability Matrix, it can be valuable to create one matrix for users with minimal experience and one for users with a lot of experience, as this can change the results substantially.

Ergonomic effort

And, of course, we have *ergonomic effort*. If you're reading this after going through the rest of the book, this will be quite familiar to you by now. Let's quickly recap the main points:

We can think of ergonomic effort as the non-learning effort required to use an interface. This effort exists throughout the interface, from the first interaction to the last, as it is baked into the interactions themselves. As users gain experience and learning effort fades, most of the remaining friction will come from this residual baseline effort. This effort continues to add up over time, with no upper limit. So for users who depend on a product throughout their day, like professional users, the cumulative effort of using it each day, several days a week, for years on end, can be *staggering*.

While users will often start with the option that requires the least learning effort, as their time spent with an interface increases, they will gravitate toward learning increasingly more ergonomic ways to accomplish their tasks. They will often be most open to more ergonomic solutions inside the products they already use (e.g., "I used to do it by hand, but now I've learned how to use the built-in automation"). However, if there is enough of an ergonomic benefit to be gained by switching to a competing product, this can be a big reason why a user will do so.

Importantly, while ergonomic effort exists in every interaction, many of the most ergonomic methods (e.g., accelerators) must be learned before a user can benefit from them. Users with heavier use cases have more motivation to overcome a lot of learning effort, while the opposite is true for users who have lighter use cases. As a result, it's critical to keep an eye on the expected frequency of use.

Whim

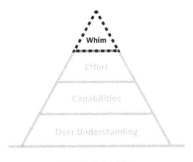

Lastly, we top off the pyramid with what we can call *whim*. I use a dashed outline here because, as we'll see, whim usually isn't real.

As you talk with users about why they chose to use one option over another, there are times when they will tell you that there was no real reason and that they just "liked one of them better than the other." In practice, though, I've found that whenever a user indicates something intangible like personal taste as the deciding factor, this is usually better accounted for by one of the other elements in this pyramid.

For example, suppose a user says they chose one option over another because they simply preferred the color of it. In that case, we can think of this as increasing their comfort level, which reduces the ergonomic effort they feel. Additionally, it may make it easier to use in certain lighting conditions—or in the case of physical products, the materials used may provide a slightly better grip with one color versus another. In cases like this, users often aren't conscious of exactly why they chose one option over the other; all they know is that they prefer it.

If you find users or people on your team ascribing a determining factor to *whim*, your ears should perk up. Take this as a sign to investigate. In practice, given the Principle of Least Effort's tendency to explain human behavior, I find that one of these other factors is almost always at play. If you can't identify the other factor on your own, gather your team and see if you can't uncover a different deciding factor as a group.

What this tool can tell us

As the Principle of Least Effort tends to be a good descriptor of user behavior, I find it's usually best to operate under the assumption that users will follow this principle *strictly* in every case. Doing so helps you test your assumptions regarding what you think you know about your users and how they see their available options.

When you believe you know what's best for these users, yet they seem to choose the "wrong option," *this is your opportunity to dig deeper.*

Because if you look closely and find that you can't account for why users would make a decision *based on what you know* about them and their options, then there's a good chance that *what you know is wrong.* Maybe this user isn't aware of what their options offer. Maybe the capabilities they need are different from what you thought. Maybe the alternative tool they're choosing has benefits you aren't yet aware of. Whatever the answer, the most valuable discoveries often come when it seems like you've reached a dead end and you bring it back to this principle.

So, when you build a product that users in your target audience aren't using, you now have a plan of attack for figuring out why. Step by step, starting at the bottom and moving up through the pyramid one level at a time, you can develop a better understanding of what's driving this behavior.

Let's walk through this process one step at a time.

Complete Goal Set

This level reminds us that users have a variety of goals they want to reach. These will influence their decisions, too. While a given app can help them reach *some* of their goals, there are always external factors at play. In other words, this tool can get you close, but it can't answer every question.

With that in mind, let's press on.

User Understanding

When talking to your target users, find people who use a competitor to your product. Always remember that your goal is *not* to convince them to use your product. Instead, you're trying to understand why they've made the decision they have.

Ask them for a list of other tools they might switch to if their preferred tool ceases to exist. This helps you get a sense of what they understand their options to be.

- **If they *do* include your tool in their list, that's a good thing.** In this case, the problem likely isn't with user understanding, so skip ahead to *capabilities*.

- **If they *don't* mention your product or say there is no other product available that does what they need it to do, it's time to dig deeper.** Ask them to be as specific as possible about why they believe those are their only suitable options.

- **If they say they have a need that your product doesn't serve, but you believe your product does, this means that one of you is mistaken, and you're one step closer to finding out why.** Try to learn as much as you can about why they believe this. After they explain, you may discover nuances they care about that you weren't including in the task you've been comparing. But if you still believe your product offers what they're looking for, demonstrate this to them and ask them if it meets their needs. (To reiterate: you're trying to *understand*, not persuade.)

- **As you do this, they may be surprised to discover that your tool does what they need it to do.** If it does, this is a problem with *user understanding*; you should improve the marketing of this element. Be sure to ask them if that was the only thing stopping them from considering it as an option. Chances are, there's more to it.

- **On the other hand, they may push back and say that the tool doesn't quite do what they need it to after receiving a demonstration.** This often points to a problem with *capabilities*, which we'll look at next.

Capabilities

When a user has a good understanding of what your product offers but decides to use a competitor, *capabilities* are the next suspect. Examine whether your product truly provides the capabilities these users need.

- **If a user tells you that a given tool doesn't do quite what they need it to, you may be very close to finding the capabilities this user needs.** Ask them to describe what exactly is missing and take special note of things like quality, format, etc. Sometimes, what users ask for in terms of capabilities can be substantial, but more often, you will discover that what you have is just a few degrees off from what they need.

- **Next, ask them if these are the only things standing between them using your product versus the product they currently use.**

- **If so, you know which capabilities you need to support to court these users.**

- **If not, then the problem likely resides with *effort*.** We'll look at that next.

Effort

When a user knows that your product has the capabilities they need, but they choose an alternative, that usually indicates that the determining factor is perceived *effort*.

- **For starters, consider *acquisition effort*.** If you have a paid product and your competition offers their product for free, that alone may be the reason. The same goes for a complicated installation process or if your product is substantially more difficult for them to get their hands on. However, this isn't a dealbreaker, as you can typically offset acquisition effort by improving ease of use.

- **Next, consider ease of use.** Remember that this contains both learning effort and ergonomic effort, and each type impacts a user differently depending on how heavy or light their use case is.

Later, create a Usability Matrix (as described in Appendix A) to compare your product to the product this user has chosen. Compare each capability that this user indicates is most important to them. Seeing where this competing product sits in the matrix will tell you something important about this user's use case. For example, suppose your product has better learnability, and the product they've chosen has better ergonomics. In that case, this can indicate that their use case is heavier than you've anticipated. This will give you a clearer picture of what you need to do to offer this type of user a superior product.

In the end, this process will help you to uncover the source of issues in your product and point you toward ways of solving them.

KEY POINTS TO REMEMBER

While it's common to say, "People use the tools that best meet their needs," I hope this gives you a better sense of how people make these kinds of decisions. Using this tool, you can more quickly determine which areas to focus on to provide a better product for the people you want to reach.

When users make choices that surprise you, this tool can help you reverse-engineer the reasons behind those choices. This enables you to make targeted improvements to offer them something more compelling. Use this to your advantage.

C

CUPID CHEAT SHEETS

Clear

How might we be discernible quickly?

1. **Make the state of the app more apparent (page 85)**

    a. Ensure that users can tell if the system is ready.

    b. Make modes more obvious.

    c. Give a clear indication of which item will be acted on.

    d. Give users a clear sense of progress.

2. **Give obvious and timely feedback (page 90)**

    a. Give feedback as quickly as you can.

    b. Be sure to send the right message.

    c. Leverage signal strength to make feedback clearer.

    d. Use previews as a form of advance feedback.

3. **Provide a distinct sense of context (page 95)**

    a. Use easily discernible structure and indicators.

    b. Ensure that users know where they are, what's ahead, and how to get back.

Unobstructed

How might we get out of the way?

1. **Reduce unnecessary delays (page 103)**

    a. Eliminate blocking transitions.

    b. Hunt down stutters and pauses.

    c. Let users leave the guided tour.

    d. Avoid controls that restrict a user's speed.

2. **Improve speed and comfort during unavoidable delays (page 108)**

    a. Leverage batching, queueing, watchers, and schedulers.

    b. Let users work in parallel during blocking tasks.

    c. Let users entertain themselves.

3. **Work with human movement (page 113)**

   a. Accommodate for physical limitations.

   b. Speed things up with multiple simultaneous inputs.

   c. Help users avoid switching input methods.

   d. Let users keep their eyes on their work.

4. **Make direct paths (page 118)**

   a. Make it possible to take shortcuts.

   b. Ensure that the important stuff is visible.

   c. Connect the dots to what users really want.

   d. Let users recycle their work.

Predictable

How might we make it possible to anticipate things?

1. **Create stable targets (page 127)**

   a. Use consistent locations for actions.

   b. Eliminate sudden layout shifts.

   c. Ensure that you don't intercept your users' inputs.

2. **Make inputs more consistent (page 132)**

   a. Treat user input the same every time.

   b. Use more reliable commands.

   c. Make use of physical controls.

3. **Produce dependable outcomes (page 137)**

   a. Offer paths to reliable results.

   b. Warn before removing capabilities.

Indulgent

How might we accept sloppier input?

1. Leverage Fitts's Law (page 144)

    a. Use larger targets.

    b. Put things closer.

    c. Simplify inputs and gestures.

2. Create more tolerant inputs (page 148)

    a. Infer what users mean.

    b. Watch out for time-limited interactions.

    c. Let users work with and around constraints.

    d. Allow for mind-changing.

Digestible

How might we reduce mental strain?

1. Let users stay mentally calibrated (page 154)

    a. Keep things in context to avoid "virtual doorways."

    b. Let users keep their momentum.

    c. Keep an eye out for distractions.

    d. Watch out for signal overload.

2. Cut down on the need to remember (page 160)

   a.   Allow for and provide contextual clues.

   b.   Make mappings familiar.

   c.   Offer direct comparisons.

   d.   Watch out for behavior that defies expectations.

3. Do the mental heavy lifting (page 165)

   a.   Allow for sorting and filtering.

   b.   Summarize with context.

4. Help users avoid pain (page 169)

   a.   Keep mental states in mind.

   b.   Introduce friction as "guardrails" where necessary.

   c.   Free your users from fear.

5. Tickle the mind with comfort (page 174)

   a.   Improve aesthetics and accommodate individual preferences.

   b.   Provide flexibility where you can.

   c.   Help users feel oddly satisfied.

C

CLEAR
Be discernible quickly

Make the state of the app more apparent
pg 85: Ensure that users can tell if the system is ready • Make modes more obvious • Give a clear indication of which item will be acted on • Give users a clear sense of progress

Give obvious and timely feedback
pg 90: Give feedback as quickly as you can • Be sure to send the right message • Leverage signal strength to make feedback clearer • Use previews as a form of advance feedback

Provide a distinct sense of context
pg 95: Use easily discernible structure and indicators • Ensure that users know where they are, what's ahead, and how to get back

U

UNOBSTRUCTED
Get out of the way

Reduce unnecessary delays
pg 103: Eliminate blocking transitions • Hunt down stutters and pauses • Let users leave the guided tour • Avoid controls that restrict a user's speed

Improve speed and comfort during unavoidable delays
pg 108: Leverage batching, queueing, watchers, and schedulers • Let users work in parallel during blocking tasks • Let users entertain themselves

Work with human movement
pg 113: Accommodate for physical limitations • Speed things up with multiple simultaneous inputs • Help users avoid switching input methods • Let users keep their eyes on their work

Make direct paths
pg 118: Make it possible to take shortcuts • Ensure that the important stuff is visible • Connect the dots to what users really want • Let users recycle their work

P

PREDICTABLE
Make it possible to anticipate things

Create stable targets
pg 127: Use consistent locations for actions • Eliminate sudden layout shifts • Ensure that you don't intercept your users' inputs

Make inputs more consistent
pg 132: Treat user input the same every time • Use more reliable commands • Make use of physical controls

Produce dependable outcomes
pg 137: Offer paths to reliable results • Warn before removing capabilities

I

INDULGENT
Accept sloppier input

Leverage Fitts's Law
pg 144: Use larger targets • Put things closer • Simplify inputs and gestures

Create more tolerant inputs
pg 148: Infer what users mean • Watch out for time-limited interactions • Let users work with and around constraints • Allow for mind-changing

D

DIGESTIBLE
Reduce mental strain

Let users stay mentally calibrated
pg 154: Keep things in context to avoid "virtual doorways" • Let users keep their momentum • Keep an eye out for distractions • Watch out for signal overload

Cut down on the need to remember
pg 160: Allow for and provide contextual clues • Make mappings familiar • Offer direct comparisons • Watch out for behavior that defies expectations

Do the mental heavy lifting
pg 165: Allow for sorting and filtering • Summarize with context

Help users avoid pain
pg 169: Keep mental states in mind • Introduce friction as "guardrails" where necessary • Free your users from fear

Tickle the mind with comfort
pg 174: Improve aesthetics and accommodate individual preferences • Provide flexibility where you can • Help users feel oddly satisfied

How to use this

This *CUPID Cheat Sheet* helps you find sources of effort that stick around permanently in an interface.

Think of this as a pre-flight checklist. Go one column at a time asking "how might we" questions. For example, for the 2nd column (U), you could start by asking "How might we reduce unnecessary delays?"

Beneath this, you'll find a list of various tactics for achieving this objective and a page # for more info.

The CUPID System from the book *Learnability Isn't Enough*
Learn more at book.hansv.com

ENJOY THIS BOOK?

If you found this helpful, I'd be honored if you could leave a quick
review. It helps out tremendously and makes it easier
for others to find the book.

Leave a review:
hansv.com/book1-review

Thank you :)

www.ingramcontent.com/pod-product-compliance
Lightning Source LLC
LaVergne TN
LVHW061955050326
832904LV00008B/286